OMAHA ORANGE

OMAHA ORANGE

A POPULAR HISTORY OF EMS IN AMERICA

CARL J. POST, Ph.D., EMT

Health Systems Management Program
New York Medical College
Valhalla, New York

JONES AND BARTLETT PUBLISHERS
BOSTON   LONDON

Editorial, Sales, and Customer Service Offices
Jones and Bartlett Publishers
20 Park Plaza
Boston, MA 02116

Library of Congress Cataloging-in-Publication Data
Post Carl J.
    Omaha orange : a popular history of EMS in America / Carl J. Post.
        p. cm.
    Includes index.
    ISBN 0-86720-187-8
    1. Emergency medical services—United States—History. I. Title.
    [DNLM: 1. Emergency Medical Services—history—United States. WX
215 P8565o]
RA645.5.P67 1992
362. 1'8'0973—dc20
DNLM/DLC
for Library of Congress   91-46513
                                                                      CIP

Cover Design: Lina Haddad
Production Services: TKM Productions

Printed in the United States of America
96 95 94 93 92   10 9 8 7 6 5 4 3 2 1

Contents

Preface

Contemporary Emergency Medical Service systems lack resources, personnel, and inventive radical minds. Survival takes priority over growth and experimentation. Medical control for these systems takes on the clear and intelligible outline of defensive medicine. Risk management is apparently a part of economic and legal concerns much more than of clinical ones. Refresher training serves to combat attrition instead of developing a basis for the expansion of manpower levels.

It translates into a situation where EMS and EMS systems are on the defensive. EMS managers have become quite reluctant to go on the offensive. Like much of American society, EMS leaders and personnel accept the notion that form is substance, as well as the related notion that process is, in and of itself, a product. The current rage has become quality assurance.

The danger of doing harm is carefully quantified, while the potential for doing some good is less often measured. Predictability suffices. Accomplishing dramatic gains with thrombolytics and twelve leads is not prudent management; research and development can be discarded in favor of alternatives, which offer no growth; ambulances do not meet specifications; radio equipment makes a mockery of supposed regulatory standards; highly placed notables consider reducing recertification requirements for volunteer personnel; and EMS itself loses credibility in one northeastern state.

The saga continues. It is almost enough to make you lose heart. EMS systems are so vitally important. How did things get to this stage? Is there anything to be done about it? Perhaps knowing the history of EMS is the first step toward finding out what can be done about its future.

EMS nearly had it all together in the late 1970s. The achievements were spectacular, and they should not remain lost or forgotten. That said, there is no disguising the fact that EMS is a divided legacy, with part of it stemming from public health and another equally awesome part coming to us by way of public safety.

Complex legacies are nothing new in the United States. Americans love to see conflicts resolved within an overall consensus. Pluralism and the need for a multitude of diverse opinions has been elevated to a national folk myth. EMS did not conform to the myth. Split loyalties, coupled with frank and mutually exclusive theories about the nature of EMS, confused outsiders and sobered insiders.

During the period between 1964 and 1990, EMS was created, brought to life, raised to the level of a national movement, left to wither without help from either a nation of volunteers or investors from the corporate sector, and finally just ignored while being allowed to rust.

It isn't at all clear that it had to come out that way. It remains unclear that EMS people and the general public should continue to accept the crushing defeat in the first part of the 1980s as a final verdict. This book has been written in the sincere hope that others who read it will come away from it eager for long-term change and immediate improvements within the EMS systems where they live.

The storied generation that persevered during almost two decades of struggle tends to fall into two broad categories: a) people who moved on to get a different job elsewhere in health care; or b) people who hung on to EMS systems as if they were haunted by a powerful dream. Certainly, almost all of them would vote to have our silly, exhilarating, bittersweet, and, at times, very sad effort to change the nature of public health and public safety made known to a wider audience.

Much of the inspiration for this book was drawn from my experiences in Kentucky, Connecticut, New York, New Jersey, Massachusetts, and Pennsylvania. Service as a consultant to both the

U.S. Public Health Service and the National Highway Traffic Safety Administration served to qualify my judgments and temper my nearly blind fanaticism. Working as a columnist for one of three major popular magazines in the field has been instructive for defining the EMS insider's quest to convert the outsiders to the EMS way of life. It may be that EMS sometimes borders on being a religious faith. If so, and I earnestly hope it is not so, then the book may offer some an exegesis, and others, a species of heresy. Either way, it is one person's attempt to describe a little-noted movement in American social, cultural, and intellectual life.

Carl J. Post, Ph.D., EMT

CHAPTER ONE

————— ✳ —————

Surfing Our Lives Away?
America in 1964

Lyndon Johnson was elected in a landslide, mouseketeers were playing bingo on beach blankets up on the silver screen, and surfing caught the imagination of the young as much as, or more than, drag racing did. Americans in their thirties or early forties grew amazed at the forces at play just over the near horizon: a burgeoning civil rights movement, the portent of a Great Society comprised of model cities, the tentative beginnings of a new, but seemingly small scale, brush fire war in Indo China, the proliferation of Leftist and alienated views among their offspring, and the phenomenal impact of "mopheads" such as the Beatles, the Searchers, the Dave Clark Five, the Rolling Stones, and Gerry and the Pacemakers on their big kahunnas and surfer girls.

The baby boom generation had reached adolescence, and nobody was too concerned about them. Most of them were well fed, the country was prosperous, and their future looked bright. Television reinforced the certainty of an American dream of sorts by featuring television shows that were more like Aesop's fables than comedies or tragicomedies. In the 1990s American primary and middle school children find solace or quality entertainment in these same shows, which appear on at least three cable stations sometimes nightly. Baby boom teeny boppers watched shows in which CIA men were the heroes of adventure pieces. Daddy's World War II inspired both dramas and comedies. If the winds of change were stirring, then veterans of the big one and their spouses could still feel secure in their country. Americans felt indomitable, invincible, and capable of fixing anything for the better.

It was at about this juncture that physicians and fire departments began to hatch paramedicine in California and southern Florida. They were, in a sense, part of a larger trend. Experimental projects in health care and other fields such as aerospace engineering were an absolute expression of a vigorous, reasonably affluent, "can do" society. Americans simply strove for perfection. Data from experiments done in conjunction with paramedicine development programs were incorporated into a large computer model at the University of California, Los Angeles, in order to monitor the evolution of clinical treatment algorithms. Eight years later, these algorithms would be amalgamated with other algorithms used for factor analysis or discriminant analysis theory. "Can do" Emergency Medical Services (EMS) began as an applied science.

More importantly, something that would later be called advanced life support was the basis for critically important, if little known, scientific endeavors in 1964. In Florida, it was also the basis for attempts to extend the physician's reach beyond the hospital via fire department personnel. Cardiac care emerged as the focal point for such efforts. Prehospital emergency care, to the extent that it had been organized, did not address traumatic injuries as the major issue.

Many writers have attributed the beginnings of all of EMS to lessons learned in the Korean War and confirmed by the Vietnamese War. While it is clear that the helicopter mania so in vogue in the 1980s may be attributable to Hawkeye Pierce and company, and that Trauma-EMS systems are one of the better known legacies of our most recent past, the fact is that trauma did not consume the EMS community's attention until the late 1970s.

In 1964, cardiac emergencies had as good a chance as trauma of being the principal emphasis within organized emergency care systems. More people are affected by heart attacks than by motor vehicle accidents or gunshot wounds. In 1964 and in the 1990s, there is a certain compelling logic to the weight of numbers. People out to save the world were not impressed by logic to any great extent. At least, in the earlier period, EMS people did not have recourse to calling everything under the sun a medical emergency. They were barely discernible throughout the American landscape.

The slate was clean. It was largely virgin turf, and anything could happen. Hospitals could reach out into their communities and provide mobile intensive care. Fire departments could mobilize to deliver first aid within the community itself and then take the patient to the hospital. A vast middle ground existed, too. Hospital-based physicians could direct a community-inspired first aid corps. Community ambulance corps could develop independently of the hospitals or the fire departments and thereby avoid medical control or accountability altogether. Most of these alternatives were not clearly played out in 1964. In some parts of the country, the ambulance doubled as a hearse. Funeral homes supplied the transportation from the accident site to the hospital in Illinois, Kentucky, New York, and elsewhere while nobody seemed to notice.

There were other things to recognize. EMS was not a strong civil rights movement. It was not part of the Great Society that Lyndon Johnson hoped to use to restructure wealth and reduce class conflict. Folk music and modern jazz both paled before the British-led resurrection of moribund American rock and roll. Television did offer two series on rival networks concerning hospital-based physicians. Medicine was not in disrepute. Richard Chamberlain gave Dr. Kildare the same heroic aura that Lew Ayres had given him in the motion pictures two decades earlier. Vince Edwards conveyed an inscrutable and omniscient style while playing Dr. Ben Casey. But the premier doctor figure on television in 1964 was a fugitive wrongly accused of killing his wife and ruefully unable to commit to anyone or anything.

Congress did not disappoint people who could make a commitment to health care. Medicare and Medicaid were created just before the dawn of an EMS era. Together Medicare and Medicaid would enable EMS to do a great deal, while at the same time prohibiting efforts by EMS to do what logically might appear to be both necessary and appropriate. A strong and solidly conceived health care finance system was created for people over a certain age. A flawed, inconsistent, and defeatist solution was doled out to the states in the hope that they would somehow pay for the needs of the sick or injured poor. Liberal states did pay, but the conservative and poor ones didn't. The poor left Mississippi for New York City, or eastern Kentucky for Detroit. Health care was just like welfare; both shifted populations and made for a raise in taxes.

A vibrant America was soon to lose its hold on certitude. An almost religious ardor for big government as the likely source of salvation for one and all was apparent everywhere. Barry Goldwater and the forerunners of the present-day moral majority were thrashed in an election that gave a halo to people openly carrying the "L" word. Liberals were in, but for how long? And what did they mean to an inchoate EMS movement?

It was hard for EMS people to know the answers to these questions. Licentiousness sometimes emerged as a synonym for liberal. Free speech, free love, and the freedom to use recreational drugs such as LSD were surfacing in American life. Poets using profanity at University of California, Berkeley, proclaimed that morals may be absolute, but ethics were situational. If it felt good, then you should at least try to do it.

The advent of improved birth control methods, coupled with the unceasing arguments of *Playboy*'s founder, Hugh Hefner, led to a more visible minority of sexually active, yet unmarried, people. American derivative gurus invited Americans to go on trips without leaving their own homes. Contemporary American language carries drug culture idoms such as "bad trip," "turn off," "tune in," and "drop out" twenty-six years later.

The National Academy of Sciences, Dr. Eugene Nagel in Miami, a group including Dr. Ron Stewart near UCLA, a cadre of dreamers in Columbus, Ohio, strident volunteers in New Jersey and elsewhere, and internists in lower Manhattan all had a different trip in mind. They wanted to combat unnecessary death as it came in the forms of car wrecks on the nation's highways, or alternatively fashionable killers that shut down the life systems of white collar executives in the city or the suburbs. Given the wide range of happenings already rattling the cages of all kinds of Americans, conquering unnecessary death had a chance to rise above the level of an abstruse fad.

Public health, public safety, cardiac, and trauma were the four major threads. Tying them together would insure the ultimate success of emergency medical services in the future. It was a legacy the baby boom generation could create for the next generation. Medicine would never be the same again. If only . . .

CHAPTER TWO

————— ✳ —————

The American Way
of Death

If you could design a surefire method for delivering high quality emergency care, would you have much of a chance of having it accepted? Would somebody's competing priorities get in your way? If you could not prove that the design was a success in a period lasting anywhere from three to seven years, would you be surprised if someone yanked the plug on the whole enterprise and caused it to collapse? Patience is not an American watchword. Timing is everything. Before turning to the EMS revolution that was born as concept in 1966, and implemented on a statewide scale as early as 1971, only to fade from view as soon as 1981, and cease to exist throughout much of the land by 1990, we should pause to examine the problem at hand. What was it that they needed so desperately to achieve? How do you insert a viable and logical approach to critical care medicine into an overheated, if not downright wasteful, health care system?

At first glance, you might surmise that 1966 and 1990 are but a little more than two decades apart. In truth, especially from an EMS standpoint, the two years are actually worlds apart. Reagan reversed the direction that the country had been heading in since 1932. Many bureaucratic layers were abolished. Much that was ridiculous and ill-conceived fell by the wayside. Some of the more poignant aspects of American life made it to the scrap heap, too. Between 1966 and 1990, it was decided that health care was not going to be an inherent right for the average citizen. The myth that health care costs could somehow be contained while maintaining a fee-for-service approach to hospital and physician charges died before Reagan even took office. Health care rationing was spoken of, written about, and even tried in places like Colorado and Oregon. There had to be several health care systems: one for the people on Medicare, another for the people who could afford to pay, still another for those qualifying for Medicaid, and, depending on your political philosophy, there could also be a group of doctors and hospital beds allocated to the medically indigent. New Jersey wound up playing Robin Hood for a time. Affluent hospitals paid a profits tax into a "superfund" in order to keep the ghetto hospitals above water. Princeton sacrificed a bit so that Newark or Camden could keep their hospitals open. It was like gouging Peter to save Paul. In 1966, Americans would have had a hard time understanding any of these problems.

"Can do" people living in a Great Society were winning the space race with the Russians. They were witnessing a baby boom generation go off to college. Civil rights were extended to African Americans on a massive scale. Poverty was confined to hillbillies, the urban poor, migrant workers, and others with handicaps to overcome. Americans spread peace all over the world by sharing their technical skills from the ranks of the Peace Corps. A domestic variant tried to do the same for both city and farm. A younger generation that had seen polio defeated by Dr. Jonas Salk had no way of knowing that they would take on AIDS about the time they were entering their forties.

America and its health care system went into a management by crisis mode between 1966 and 1990. Debts accumulated and assets depreciated. The insurance companies found it impossible to pay for 80 percent of most hospital bills. The legal climate mandated numerous tests for many types of patients, and they were performed under the guise of defensive medicine. The patient was a potential adversary. Malpractice insurance premiums grew to such a point that they were a dissuasion to a career in medicine. Technology meant a competitive edge for the recruiting hospital as much or more than it meant a boon to definitive patient care. Expansion by the bigger hospitals led to regulatory overreaction. Beds were closed while healthy Americans got older. In 1990, years of health planning and resource development had resulted in a lack of beds. Hospitals were already filled. EMS people were diverted from one emergency room to the next, and their patients lay in the back rig hoping to win at patient placement roulette.

On the other hand, in the 1990s, it is hard to remember the time when health care was energized by a kind of relentless optimism. Folks had reference to two documents. Both of them decried the senseless deaths of Americans from traumas and trauma-related medical emergencies. From the sixties came the discussion of accidental death and disability—a neglected disease. From the eighties came in turn a lucid analysis of injuries within the United States. The message was the same. Nothing had changed, or so it seemed. The things that had been changed soon reverted to an earlier form or no form at all.

September 17, 1989, Philadelphia, Pennsylvania—there is a huge parade. The people are busy celebrating the 200th anniversary of the American Constitution. The document provides them with a Bill of Rights. They are entitled to free speech, the right of assembly, and a number of other essential freedoms that are so commonplace in American life.

Paramedics in that same city can take as long as 38 minutes to bring a serious patient to a hospital for definitive care. The patient has no constitutionally-guaranteed right to emergency care. Americans have never had the clear right to obtain quality health care. Emergency care in a free and pluralistic society is a difficult proposition at best. It becomes something far worse in the face of health care rationing, AIDS hysteria, and a growing failure of nerve at the national level.

Americans had tried to build a rather impressive national Emergency Medical Services system from 1974 through 1982. The fact that it failed to survive constitutes a tragedy. Tragedies have their moments: some of them inspiring, others are comedic, and still others, epic or transcendental. Maybe that is why the ancient Greeks valued them.

Eight years of American EMS history have to have meant something. Even more so because organized efforts to foster the development of viable emergency care throughout the United States were unheard of before 1966. In that year, the National Academy of Sciences discovered that Americans died much too often from accidents, and as a result studies were commissioned. In time, these were followed by experiments involving new ideas sanctioned to take place in Jacksonville, Florida, in Illinois (see Chapters 3, 7, and 9), and in the suburbs east of New York City.

The experiments went well, or so it seemed at the time. Something tangible had a slight chance of passing the deliberation of the American Congress. It might even get past the presidential veto phase. Public Law 93-154 became a reality in 1973 as oil prices went up and "peace with honor" in Vietnam was followed by a recession. The EMSS Act (Emergency Medical Services Systems), an act that was expanded upon by subsequent public laws (94-573 in 1976 and 96-142 in 1979), established a national lead agency for the purpose of improving emergency care. Monies in excess of one hundred eighty-five million dollars were slated for a brand new misadventure in the realm of federal government interference with the flow of cash to each of the fifty states. Sixty million dollars a year, each year, for at least three years? The need for fewer accidental deaths had given rise to another sinew in the layers of bureaucracy. The scenario was an all too familiar one, but this particular agency was destined to be something far different from its sister agencies (see Chapters 7 and 9).

Passing along dollars to the fifty individual states had already become a time-honored convention. From the time of Andrew Jackson through to John F. Kennedy and Lyndon Baines Johnson, the golden rule had been applied to development and patronage activities: "He who has the gold makes the rules!" The Feds passed out goodies or allowed them to trickle down to the less fortunate among the bidders for favor. The process had been accelerated during the presidency of Franklin D. Roosevelt. In the thirties and also during the forties, people turned to the government for answers and sustenance. This trend was partially arrested under Eisenhower in the fifties, but the sixties made up for that with a vengeance. Formulas to make grants more scientific came into vogue at that time. EMSS was a late addition to the formulas.

Title 12 was the bureaucratic cipher assigned to the EMSS administration in Washington, DC. EMS folks were entitled to try whatever it was that they managed to cook up. Health planning underwent a similar conversion into layers of functionaries via legislation-creating health systems agencies. The seventies saw federal programs being implemented locally. This could mean that power and money would be passed into the hands of innocuous mandarins, who would translate the federal thrust into a more palatable local idiom and thereby adumbrate it, or the right special interests could distort the actual mission of the program and deftly plan to fail. Pork barrel tactics made it in the South. Slovenly organized regional implementation schemes might result in funds for new ambulances or radios without having needless reference to hindering paperwork such as mission statements. It was all one big game. It has always been that way. It was as it was supposed to be.

If the need for fewer accidental deaths had given rise to another bureaucracy, and the scenario had all the makings of an all too familiar course of events, then this particular agency was destined to be something far different. An unanswered question is whether this agency—the Division of Emergency Medical Services (DEMS) of the Department of Health, Education and Welfare—really had a chance to accomplish its stated goal of making America a nation blanketed by wall-to-wall EMS regions, totalling 304 from coast to coast and beyond. Can anyone imagine a uniform approach to a pivotal problem taking the same form in all fifty states? Unlike France, in America, departments have to intrude upon several layers of state, county, municipal subdivisions, and incorporated villages just to get a policy implemented. Hence the basic wisdom of the golden rule applies. Federal officials had to bribe and cajole their way to grass roots compliance with ambulance standards, which would become baseline definition sets for Emergency Medical Technician training. The problems encountered by DEMS blunted the effectiveness of its fourth cousin agency, the National Highway Traffic Safety Administration, as well (see Chapters 4, 8, and 10). EMS leaders were throwing sand up against the tide—a tide that ran against big government and reached flood stage with the election of Ronald Reagan.

Zeal bordering on fanaticism was the only weapon that the DEMS functionaries and their assorted grantees had available to them for resisting the disintegration of society, in which the central government had long played a leading role. A formula of sorts was used to mask a burning determination to make sure that needless deaths were prevented or virtually eliminated. It came down to anointing area hospitals as trauma centers, spinal cord centers, burn centers, poison centers, high risk infant centers, and cardiac centers. Five to fifteen percent of the cases in each of these categories had to receive the highest level of care. Resource hospitals played traffic cop for patients bound for any of these centers. The rules of the road were found in the regional medical control plan. Who went where, and why, were the four Ws of EMS systemization. Radios and incident/encounter forms tracked patients through the system. Hospitals went along with it to some extent because of the uplifting effects of the golden rule.

The DEMS people wanted to ignore local traditions and parochial interests in order to impose on everyone this simple paradigm for the eradication of unnecessary death. Market shares were to be discarded, proprietary interests had to get out of the way or sing a different tune, and monies were passed out in the expectation that its recipients would at least try to conform to the DEMS ideal. After seven years of struggle, and an unfavorable reputation with the Office of Management and Budget, and many key Senators and members of Congress, the DEMS people had obtained functional compliance in about half of the nation's 304 EMS regions. Structured health care delivery could evolve from its most basic level in many different areas of the country.

"Could" means "maybe"; evolve means getting it together. DEMS may or may not have put all the pieces together in the area of structured health care delivery. Visionaries do not captivate everyone. Zealots do not always eliminate the skepticism and unbridled agnosticism left behind when the crusade is over. A few of the crusaders now and again slip down into the ranks of the fallen, too.

All along the way, there are those who merely pretend to implement formulas for change. In Connecticut, they might suggest that Catholic mothers must have their babies in Catholic hospitals. Influential leaders might intimate that Baptist mothers had to do the same thing in Tennessee. The locals needed concrete incentives to go through the motions of supporting resource hospitals, trauma centers, and somebody else's version of EMT training. Local ambulance services were seldom privy to the operational implications of the regional medical control plans. Local physicians' councils contrived to disagree over such matters as mercury levels in the context of transport criteria.

Selfish criticisms brought on defensiveness within the ranks of DEMS. Tons of information and research were employed to counter the arguments of those who had yet to gravitate to the true faith. The information proved that DEMS had erected systems capable of delivering basic life support. DEMS was incapable of proving anything more. In 1981, advanced life support was still making progress on various drawing boards throughout the country. It did not work as such anywhere at all. Studies funded by the Department of Transportation echoed the findings of those required by DEMS. Paramedics managed to keep very critical patients alive long enough to die in the hospital rather than outside of it. EMS, as often as not, merely served to change the place where the patient died. Systems without advanced life support capability did as well as or better than systems with that capability. The locals had provoked a learned reaction, the reaction had inspired a lively definition process, and the process culminated in a bureaucratic and institutional nightmare. The DEMS formula was supposed to have been finished at the local level when the EMSS manifested clear and indisputable advanced life support capabilities. In actual practice, the EMSS region was as done as it was ever going to be for 1981 when it achieved basic life support proficiency.

DEMS came up with half a loaf at exactly the wrong time. Americans were experiencing some other revolutions in the popular mind from 1974–1981. Liberal, idealistic, and selfless attitudes were a thing of the past. "Volunteer" took on a new and more menacing connotation. Big government was suddenly under attack, and America reversed its course for the first time since 1934. A movie actor sought the presidency for the very purpose of doing away with formulas, resource hospitals, and medical control plans. Standards imposed from on high were automatically construed as inherently evil.

The same movie actor would be saved from a gunshot wound in what DEMS had codified as being a trauma center. Ronald Reagan vetoed specialty center funding six months after his brush with death. A board was established especially for emergency medicine as most Americans focused on their fellow citizens held captive in Iran and the deficit in the national budget. Americans had elected a leader with little taste for Washington-based programs that drew support from tax dollars. Reagan meant change; his presidency was a watershed in the nation's history. Social programs so typical of American domestic policy since 1933 were under the gun. Free enterprise was the salvation offered to one and all. Real needs were to be met by voluntary efforts or the partnership between the government and private industry. Guerilla wars in Central America took the front seat in policy matters. Liberal catechisms went up in smoke. Educational reform, racial harmony, and urban relief provided the first set of ashes.

The health care situation went largely unnoticed during the first months of the new order. An invidious and tortured assault on health care policy was yet to be unleashed. DEMS still existed in 1981, and the formulas lived on for the time being. The majority of the energies devoted to continuing the DEMS campaign to create EMSS regions with the capability to provide solid basic life support were devoted to trauma and trauma-EMS systems. The formulas were factored to include one independent variable—the trauma center.

Refocusing of activities around just one disease had the virtue of simplifying the argument. Trauma centers would come first and then there would be time for resource coordination and determinations of compliance. The new regime saw things differently. Budget-balancing accountants had already given rise to something known as Reaganomics. Popular support for EMS systems must have been building up over the seven years of the Title 12 program. They reasoned that the reservoir of EMS support could be tapped to sustain EMSS regions without the benefit of a Division of Emergency Medical Services within the Department of Health, Education, and Welfare. Block grant awards might help, too. The government would cooperate with business and rely on volunteers, while EMS competed with rat control and rape prevention programs for increasingly scant socially aware dollars.

Ronald Reagan effectively demolished the experiment in logical emergency care delivery on a nationwide basis by dismissing its leader, working behind the scenes in Congress to thwart a last minute bid to renew the legislative authority for DEMS and more passthroughs, and confining the remaining government agency efforts to coordination of state and local activities. True believers were relegated to emergency rooms, trauma intensive care units, or ambulance driving. DEMS's future was questionable. EMS was still an important cause for old allies like Senator Edward Kennedy, but dreams of Camelot had faded by now. "No government" was considered "good government." It may not have mattered in some hearts and minds. Key people in the EMS community celebrated a new era of laissez faire. They were free to follow the local and parochial way, or to divorce the ambulance industry from the hospital phase of care, or to assume that EMS was pretty much analogous to a phone company or electric company and sell it as a legal monopoly to towns and counties for three to five years.

There were two fundamental misconceptions associated with their jubilation: 1) no amount of celebrating could blot out the omnipresent Health Care Finance Administration; 2) the public had other things on its mind. The financial authorities could, and still do, trammel upstart ambulance providers. The collapse of the nationwide effort led quickly to diminished activity at all levels. The golden rule did not apply when there was no gold left to prime the pump.

Title 12-style EMS survived in pockets all over the United States. The remaining EMS regions gathered in Virginia every year to pass around the cup of hemlock and think about what might have been (about 50 or so out of the original 304 survived into the late 1980s). The country moved toward health care rationing. A concept known as diagnosis-related groups was perfected in New Jersey and four other states with a bit of help from Yale's School of Medicine. It was meant to create a new situation in which hospitals and physicians would be both efficient and accountable. It misfired badly. Patients were sent home sooner and sicker in a mistaken stab at imposed economies of scale. Critics remarked that the change translated into a system where substandard care was rendered under the effects of average prices.

The impact of diagnosis-related groups (DRGs) on EMS was enormous. Poor people were taken to public hospitals and left to die there in holding rooms. The insured rich and middle class people were taken to trauma and burn specialty centers for definitive care because there would be a greater likelihood that the patient might survive long enough to qualify the receiving facility for (DRG) reimbursement. American television news cameras highlighted the implicit genocide of public versus private hospitals in Dallas, Texas. In one of its February 1985 issues, the *New England*

Journal of Medicine was forced to editorialize that hospitals were for patients, too. Economic diversion was the symbol the public noticed on the television screen.

American EMS people were trying to expand their horizons and improve their capabilities at a time when the country was undergoing a wider number of changes. The political, economic, and cultural climate changed a great deal between 1966 and 1990. EMS grew in scope and size between 1974 and 1981, and it has not grown very much since that time. It just may be that the deck was stacked against the missionaries at DEMS. Fate, history, or the gods foreordained that the DEMS folks were born a bit too late to change the EMS world. The formula, the standard, and the plan for critical care medicine may well deserve to gather dust in the few remaining EMS archives.

It is certain that traumatic injuries are still as big a problem as they were when the National Academy of Sciences called attention to them in 1966. America has come full circle in that respect. There are more paramedics, and better cardiac care looms over the horizon. EMS is ripe for another attempt at regionalized emergency care according to normative national standards. It might be an entirely new revolution brought forth by a new DEMS. It could also take the form of a renaissance brought into being by several segments of the EMS community. The old revolution was a meaningful example. In the next chapter, it is examined against the background of the time in which it began.

CHAPTER THREE

———— ✳ ————

A Revolution Approaches: 1965–1974

Americans grew ever more unsettled as the baby boom generation hit high school age. Plans for college were made in many middle class households. Male applicants worried about SAT scores, but also worried about their number in the draft lottery. The quick, certain, and decisive, yet undeclared, war in Southeast Asia was a continual source of frustration and despair. The media served napalm on the television right around dinner time each night. It reached the boiling point in 1968 when the television media exploded the deeply held myth of a light at the end of the tunnel, which manifested itself all over South Vietnam. The vast majority of Americans sat by their dinner tables in bewilderment as the Communists fought American soldiers to a standstill for a little more than three weeks.

The Great Society went up in flames as African Americans rejected Big Government's helping hand as the outreach of a thinly disguised overseer out to make them Uncle Toms. Olympic athletes echoed the rejection of mainstream American values voiced during widespread urban riots. From Gary, Indiana to Plainfield, New Jersey, it became clear that model cities were hard to come by and even harder to maintain under widespread urban blight. An epic flight to the suburbs had begun, which left EMS people, doctors, and hospital administrators with a lot more planning to do.

The baby boomers had a foreign war on their hands, and a second war was beginning on the home front. Campus protests against the war sometimes blended into the background of social and racial protests. Many Americans "mobilized" to stop the war and racism, while upper middle class whites worried about their less fortunate sisters and brothers.

They sometimes worried in Granny glasses made popular by the folksounding rock group known as The Byrds. At other times, they worried while expanding their minds with green, gold, or red marijuana. More tortured souls escaped these concerns entirely through speed, acid, or a lethal combination of the two known as DMT. Motherhood, togetherness, and a two-car garage had given way to "tuning in" or "turning on" while dropping out of the mainstream.

Anxiety over the war, the draft, and those gnawing doubts about this being the wonderful universe Mommy and Daddy had planned for and promised all began to undercut the invincible "can do" mindset at play in America from 1960 through 1965. At times, the teenagers lapsed into a "live for today and forget about tomorrow" frame of mind. Free love scored more than a few hits. People made love to one another in order to prove they existed. Conventional morality paled before braless women, long-haired men, and workable birth control devices such as the pill.

Hugh Hefner had argued that sex was an enjoyable pastime that came to humans naturally. Fear of death and fear that maybe we "can't do" made this argument easier to take. It would be wrong to ascribe some harmful intent to Mr. Hefner. His conspicuous effort to revitalize the animal side of us had its roots in the belief that the "can do" society was sexually repressed and therefore unhealthy. His qualified success in this area was not so much a symptom of a return to Hedonism as it was a clear indication that the old certitude underlying the old confidence in American life was coming unglued.

Parents had to contend with long-haired boys and girls lacking traditional underwear. Flowers were worn by a large minority of children as a repudiation of war and weapons. Strange-looking people got haircuts and sometimes shaved to be "Clean for Gene," as they supported Senator Eugene McCarthy's bid for the Democratic nomination for President during the primaries held in 1968.

When he lost, many reverted to the old form—beads, ponchos, recreational drugs, and sex—or a more intense form—armed strife replete with combat medics characterized the flower children's assault on the Democratic Convention in Chicago just a few months later.

The older folks, the generation that had beaten Hitler and Tojo, now had to watch many of their offspring repudiate them, their culture, and the idea of war entirely. A counterculture shouted that America was insane, mercenary, criminal, and much too uptight. It offered myriad criticisms, proposed few, if any, solutions, and left the Boomers and their parents confused, befuddled, and without a clue as to why everyone in the mainstream had to feel guilty.

Robert Kennedy and Martin Luther King each had been murdered as they tried to heal the nation in 1968. A rather brilliant, if thoroughly unpleasant, leader took their place. Health care and even a considerable amount of what Americans would come to call EMS was possible after a quasi-reactionary government headed by Richard M. Nixon took office.

There were, however, some things that the new regime did not seem to have a definite handle on. The war continued and, in fact, got worse, extending to more countries and involving massive, yet seemingly indiscriminant, bombing. Bad episodes such as the full-scale massacre of a village of Vietnamese civilians, the random napalm injury of a ten-year-old girl, and the execution of a captured enemy point blank in the forehead by an officer in the army of our client state got a disproportionate amount of press and air play. Presidential commission members studied the social and racial problems of America to the point of distraction, only to come up with a huge whitewash that hid a multitude of sins. There were practical limits to what the government and the society it administered could do or hope to do. Nobody, except for some extreme radicals, wanted to redistribute the wealth evenly throughout the land. The middle class had sustained severe hits as a direct result of taxes levied to support President Johnson's not-so-miraculous programs, which is one reason they repudiated the Democrats in the 1968 election in favor of a man who promised he had a plan.

Richard M. Nixon was both a complex genius and a self-deprecating person who wanted affection but could never fully accept it when he got it. America under Nixon did not eventuate in a situation in which the government washed its hands of a number of its social responsibilities. Nixon's America still used planning. The federal government persisted in playing a role it had played since the New Deal of 1933. The government would, as before, intervene in the private lives of Americans in a way that was presumed to be beneficial to them. It would also play a leading, though cautious, role in the development and expansion of the nation's health care system. Health care was a right, not a commodity, available only to the well-to-do. Finishing the American health care delivery system remained on a list of tasks that President Nixon would have to address during an administration largely concerned with war abroad, civil unrest at home, and harnessing the energies of a putative silent majority. Such measures were intended to deflect the massive insult put forward by the flower children and their allies among the press, clergy, academe, and the civil rights enthusiasts.

National health insurance came extraordinarily close to existence in 1973. However, Nixon's impeachment scuttled a deal between industry and labor that had been evolved over the course of Nixon's first term. Health Maintenance Organizations were attempted on a large scale following the Kaiser Permanente model popularized by years of success in California. Regional medical programs were implemented between 1970 and 1972. These short-lived "can do" oriented social experiments came into play just as the Vietnam War was losing its earlier confines extending into Laos and, more horribly, into Cambodia. About eleven million dollars was spent on EMS experimentation within the context of federal efforts to redistribute, organize, and develop a logic for existing health care resources.

Nobody was actually sure whether EMS was part of the injury control/injury prevention campaign which was gaining momentum under the auspices of the Department of Transportation's National Highway Traffic Safety Administration, or whether it belonged with the visionaries who were articulating rural health care, logical strategies for determining the need for health services, and universal health care for everyone without reference to their ability to pay. In truth, EMS was emerging as something that was going to encompass a little bit of all those things. If very few people knew what EMS was, then everybody seemed convinced somehow that America needed it. The National Academy of Sciences had, after all, pronounced traumas and trauma-related medical emergencies a neglected disease while Lyndon Baines Johnson was still relatively popular. Naturally, back in 1966, before the torching of the model cities, and two years before the huge Communist attack, therefore ruefully recalled as the Tet Offensive, the "can do" Americans could, or thought they could, make America, the world, and EMS better.

The support of the federal government, highway safety engineers, public safety authorities, and academic, real world physicians would not have been enough to sustain EMS as a vital new concept without there being a certain intrinsic merit to EMS in and of itself. Charitable foundations got involved. The Robert Wood Johnson Foundation would spend part of the next decade improving EMS communications in the hope that forty-four areas would benefit from these efforts and evolve into a somewhat systematic delivery organization. People at Ohio State University and in the surrounding community of Columbus, Ohio, built their own delivery mechanism more or less from scratch, brooking neither dollars nor interference from the federal government. Anti-war protests, and the rise of militant feminism did not keep the small-but-growing emergency medical services system movement from making careful progress. The generation gap fomented by war, changing mores and a feeling of betrayal on both sides of the gap, had little impact on emergency care development activities. If health care was at that time an accepted right, then broadening its compass was both logical and appropriate—at least in theory.

Isolated pockets of EMS began to sprout throughout the land— on Cape Cod, in southern Florida, in southern California, in lower Manhattan, in northeastern New Jersey, and even in the blighted poor white area known as Appalachia. Anything bigger than that required demonstrable proof that EMS was not a fad. Did it make a difference? Would it do any good? Could Americans come up with something as viable and powerful as the paramedical program created by Dr. Frank Pantridge in Belfast while in the midst of a civil war?

The Nixon Administration wanted to know if "can do" meant "would do." Training and systems development schemes were funded on a pilot basis. The monetary total was sixteen million dollars. Some of it went to Baltimore and northern Arizona for work with

communications. The majority of it was allocated to system develop-
ers. Grantees included Arkansas, which proved to be a breeding
ground for articulate antagonists, a three county area including San
Diego, California, a seven county area centering on Jacksonville,
Florida (where neat paradigms about patient transfers to hospitals
took a while to sink in), southeastern Ohio centering on the college
town of Athens, and Illinois, which saw David R. Boyd, MDCM
conceive a pyramid of hospital care levels and an analogous pyramid of patient care needs. For Boyd, working in Illinois as a de facto
statewide EMS director after a stint in a trauma unit in Chicago, and
some formative experiences at Dr. R. A. Cowley's Shocktrauma
Hospital in Baltimore, EMS meant matching those most in need
with those most capable of caring for that need. Some research in
the Mount Vernon area of the state would eventually show that the
idea of giving both the patient and the potential receiving hospital
a figurative report card facilitating the matching process worked
well for blunt trauma cases. It was a striking example of "can do"
ingenuity in unsettled times.

David R. Boyd, MDCM was to become the single most important figure in EMS history between 1964 and 1990 (see Chapters 6
and 9). He built a comprehensive and internally consistent emergency care system on a statewide basis. In effect, he had proven in
short order that health care might indeed be logical and some of its
results should be predictable. His war on unnecessary death was
also a battle against duplicative hospital services, overbedded or
substandard facilities, and excessive medical testing.

Boyd's brand of EMS was nothing short of a revolution. It
offered a challenge to the established order of things. Structure was
bad enough, and clearly defined echelons of care weren't much
better, but was there a clear logic underlying the placement of
emergent critical patients? It all added up to a threat to the community, its hospitals, the physicians working there, and the established
EMS non-system. EMS as propounded by Boyd in Illnois, and later
on a nationwide scale, meant revolutionary change.

If Robert Wood Johnson funded peaceful evolution within the
context of established community, and if DOT-NHTSA financed
vehicle and training improvements as it still does today, then Boyd
at the state and national levels offered a devastating critique of
orderless acute care and disorganized prehospital care, as either of

them pertained to EMS. Critics in Pittsburgh and Dallas would later holler that there were other mousetraps—mousetraps almost as good. But Boyd got there first, and many people even today would opine as to who got there best. It was by no means an easy trip. Nixon tried to kill legislation for an EMS authority at the national level (see Chapter 9). He did not succeed. At first, the new agency lacked dramatic leadership. Almost inevitably, the helm fell to the radical in Illinois who had done so much in such a short time. Boyd wanted to agitate for change, growth, and systems development.

At almost the same time, Nixon was fired and Gerry Ford became our best known unelected president. We won the overseas war, or so the experts say, but we pulled out of that theatre of operations effectively losing the peace that followed. Americans have felt varying degrees of guilt, confusion, and frustration over the war ever since. America was slowly losing its "can do" perspective. A post war recession didn't contribute anything toward the preservation of the tangible remnants of such a perspective. Alienated Lefists felt vindicated by the collaspe of Nixon and the war effort. Racial tension was met with much improved SWAT capabilities within the police departments of many American cities. Maybe the EMS revolution was simply born too late? Just as everything else began to come apart in "can do" America, Dr. Boyd offered a useful, balanced, and workable restructuring of hospitals and ambulances, and the way each did business. Would 1964 have been a more auspicious time? A decade or so later, EMS was putting out "can do" noises and hoping a shaken society would want to buy into those noises and the lifesaving changes they represented.

Revolutions can be conservative in nature. They can preserve or restore values and structures that were lost. Boyd's EMS wanted to take hospitals and specialty care physicians beyond Medicare, Medicaid, an excess of hospital testing to a time where severity of illness and injury dictated the appropriateness of hospital placement, hospital transfer, and critical care staffing patterns. Systems were popular among managers and the information sciences throughout the seventies. Planning matrices kept thousands of public health graduate students busy en route to an MPH and a job with a planning agency. Physicians in Washington, DC preached the doctrine of consumerism in purchasing medicines and prescriptive drugs. Patients were to be "activated." "Can doisms" died hard. The

radical from Illinois could get by without attracting too much attention from the huge, non-EMS, non-hospital, non-public-safety majority in this country. EMS could have been just another workable
fad such as neighborhood health centers or generic drug catalogs.
The radical wanted to change things for what seemed to be the
better.

American EMS and America itself were about to be challenged.
Nothing would ever be quite the same again. The meaningful restructuring of everything had to survive the end of "can do," the
narrowly conceived health care mandates of the Reagan years, a loss
of interest within the general public, and, worst of all, ineluctable
divisiveness within the EMS world itself.

EMS was comprised of many elements, and it still is today. Four
principal orientations have been predominant: trauma, cardiac,
public health, and public safety. Any of these orientations might in
turn have a dichotomy between paid and volunteer elements. An
examination of each group and the role it played in dooming or
supporting organized emergency care from the early days until the
Bush Administration is presented in the chapters that follow (see
Chapters 4, 5, 7, and 8 in particular).

CHAPTER FOUR

————— ✳ —————

Transportation—From the Community to the Hospital

Community based EMS providers often use authorized vehicles to transport the sick and injured to a higher level of care. In Maine, New Hampshire, and parts of the deep South, an EMS person gets to the scene before a specially dedicated vehicle can arrive. These EMS people are known as "fast squads." They take the place of ambulances in the short term by working on and with the patient until a modern-day ambulance arrives. This can take as long as thirty to forty-five minutes. Citizens residing in at least thirty small New England towns are accustomed to this arrangement. They realize that they cannot afford to buy such $90,000 to $140,000 luxury items for their individual towns; the call volume is too low. A cadre of trained personnel on stand-by would be difficult to come by. There is the national ski patrol at the nearby resort, and local, isolated colleges might have developed medical responsibility, but ambulance service as such is not automatic in this part of the country. Extending care prior to dispatching an ambulance becomes a clear medical priority under such circumstances.

Humans should be able to depend on fixed-wing aircraft, helicopters, mobile intensive care units, ALS configured ambulances, BLS configured ambulances, or the four-wheel drive vehicles used by EMT-Ds and other types of first responders. More elegant or discriminating tastes might run to a real or imagined need for Mobile Emergency Room Vans, the purportedly "A-bomb resistant" mobile homes dedicated to disaster coordination, BLS-configured primary care ambulances that never transport, but sometimes bring the summons for EMS system abuse, or lastly, paramedic supervisor four-wheel drive vehicles that carry no medications and have zero capacity for linking on-site to hospital communications. The unit, the rig, or the bus are, to varying degrees, fundamental elements within Emergency Medical Services in America circa 1990.

Travel is a significant aspect of American culture. Americans linked their coasts in the previous century by using railroads. At the beginning of the present century, Henry Ford democratized travel by producing low cost but durable automobiles. Individual or family ownership of a motor vehicle has been something of a norm in this country since the end of World War II, while air travel has become an attractive alternative for businesspeople since the sixties.

Beginning with the dust bowls of Oklahoma in the 1930s, and carrying through to their computer industry equivalents near Boston in 1990, the ability to travel has given individuals and whole families the right to absent themselves from a hostile business climate or a polluted environment. The road leads to a figurative land of milk and honey, or so it seems. A vehicle is a badge of status. It supports our claims to individuality, be it through political bumper stickers, neon windshield wipers, or a host of little stuffed animals clinging to the window.

But is the vehicle much more than a tool? Can an ambulance alone suffice to create an EMS delivery system? Does the crew of the ambulance, no matter how well trained, really figure in the deliberations and machinations that go on beyond the entrance to a critical care hold area? It is certain that ambulances with properly trained crews make many kinds of EMS activities possible.

In the sixties, and throughout much of the seventies, the Department of Transportation provided monies for the purchase of ambulances at the grass roots level. Ambulances did not spring like magic from fire departments or funeral homes. Real, legitimate, and bona fide patient care transportation had to be created. The community, armed with a desire for at least some EMS, sought out the appropriate benefactor within the Big Government in order to get a vehicle. What it would carry and what level of personnel should staff it was, and sometimes still is, the subject of much debate.

There was no denying the fact that many people possessed a "gut" feeling that their town had to have at least one. Some might have been horrified to learn that New Jersey was estimated to have no less than eleven hundred ambulances in the middle of the seventies, despite the fact that it was the fourth smallest and most densely populated state in the union. Bruce Springsteen or Eddie and the Cruisers had more ambulances available to them at the Jersey Shore than were available in Nebraska, Oklahoma, Arkansas, and Tennessee combined. Being born to drag race near the New Jersey coast was safer than running a trailer truck across what became the interstate highway system. On average, ambulances were scarce resources in the sixties.

Even before anything like a meaningful delivery system was in place, it soon became clear to analysts from DOT, the Robert Wood Johnson Foundation, the regional medical programs, and, a bit later, Dr. David R. Boyd's DEMS that urban and densely populated areas demanded or purchased the biggest portions of the known supply of ambulances. The ambulance, as opposed to the police car or the hearse, symbolized EMS in the smaller communities where there had never been a rig before. Not surprisingly, the Feds tried to get everyone throughout the land to use white-colored vehicles, which were trimmed in Omaha orange and decorated by a 360 degree Aesculapian Star square on both the left and right side panels. The rig was the symbol of a nationally standardized emergency care method trickling down to the home folks.

People living between Boston and Washington, DC would have had a hard time imagining just how impressive the sight of such a rig emerging out of the morning mists could have been for patients and their families near Clarksburg, West Virginia. Nor could they fairly consider the impact of an entire fleet of them operating, though briefly, in and around Lexington, Kentucky. Units that were readily distinguishable from funeral home vehicles meant change. It meant systemization at work. It might have also been construed as Big Brother in Washington, DC interfering yet again in the doings of honest-to-God Americans trying to mind their own business.

Fortunately, some of the vehicles came from sources quite apart from the Feds. Commercial ambulance services already had the basis for a specialized fleet of vehicles situated in many of the larger American cities. Fire department involvement in what seemed to many a rather natural extension of the public safety functions

grew more pronounced between 1964 and the late eighties. Indig-
enous civic organizations often allied with volunteer fire departments under the auspices of rescue squads—rescue sometimes ne-
cessitating an ambulance and clinical skills a bit beyond rudimentary
first aid for the rescuers. Professional ambulance drivers and volunteer ambulance drivers alike elicited a critical public acceptance.
Very few members of either group would have eagerly subscribed to
the notion that they were somehow destined to be part of a national
movement, let alone the idea that all ambulances had to be decked
out in Omaha orange, white, and blue.

If you asked the average citizen in 1964, or in 1992, whether a
paramedic was pretty much an ambulance driver, what do you think
the response might be? And realizing, of course, that the reverse
might be equally regarded as true, are all ambulance personnel who
are covered in the local area gazette de facto paramedics? EMS at its
crudest could be explained by the idea of a rig taking a patient from
the community to the hospital. History, or what often passes for it,
might support that view up to a point.

After all, they had ambulances during the Civil War and even
earlier. But was the first instance of modern trench warfare, replete
with human wave attacks, remotely comparable to civilian life at that
time? Did the military model extend into the mainstream in the two
or three decades after the war? Did "gut shot" patients survive? Did
the ambulance merely facilitate changing the place where they
died? The French used airborne and ground ambulances five years
later to remove the wounded from the battlefields dominated by
the Prussians, and in so doing were following the example handed
down by Napoleon Bonaparte. But were French civilians burned as
badly in their private lives as soldiers hit by shell fragments? Could
they endure multiple penetrating traumas from bolt action, breech-
loading rifles first used by the Prussians at Sedan? Was Napoleon III
personally at risk in the average French community? Modern-day
popes are shadowed by a team of surgeons in a mobile operating
room. Does the average Italian have traumatologists at his beck and
call?

It remains that organized emergency care delivery systems are
heavily locked into transportation. If you trained seventy-five percent of a medium-sized city's population in first aid/CPR, or even
smart defibrillation, then you might still need a dedicated vehicle

with crews capable of IV therapy, intubation, or the strategic placement of a needle in the chest every once in a while. System builders
at all levels found the going tough when there weren't enough
ambulances available. Dispatching and initial stabilization points
can only go so far. If a rig is not a system, then it is difficult to have a
system without one. Time is distance. Care delayed can become care
denied. Getting a patient to the appropriate physician, facility, or
supercenter is often the ultimate hurdle, and a rig is normally
involved. It need not come from the community to the hospital.
There are instances, as we shall see in the next chapter, where it
always was, and still is, the other way around.

CHAPTER FIVE

———— ✳ ————

Critical Care—From the Hospital to the Community

The short-lived EMS revolution began in 1966. It reached its height with Dr. David R. Boyd and his DEMS organization distributing hundreds of millions of dollars from 1973 to 1981. It came to an abrupt end in 1982. It was as if a series of massive waves had flooded coastal beachfront areas only to recede when the weather cleared and the winds died down.

Unfortunately, flood tides are seldom completely spontaneous phenomena. EMS funding, however, is not as predictable. The potency of the U.S. Public Health Service's Division of Emergency Medical Services owes more than a little to a public health thread in EMS that was unmistakable after 1970 when the health care dollars for EMS started with the regional medical programs. The winds of change that had inspired efforts to concoct working models of regionalized emergency care did not die down until a few years after the demise of the Title 12 program in 1982. Health care dollars still went to EMS from 1983 through 1985 under the auspices of Preventive Health Block Grants. The monies were insufficient and insignificant, but EMS had a hold on the minds of the public health people and drew nourishment from the abundant health care dollars that were administered longer than it took to play out a bureaucrat's five- or seven-year plan. How did EMS marshal more than a decade of public health concern and untold wealth for disbursement throughout the entire country?

The answer lies in the fact that EMS systemization was caught up in a larger scheme of things. EMS was and is comprised of many elements. Critical care medicine should be one of the most important of those elements. Critical care involves hospitals. Analysts and economists lump all hospitals together under the banner of an acute care sector. This notion forms a major factor to be examined in our treatment of the topic of critical care as it affects EMS development. The other major factor in critical care medicine involves the concept of caregiving. Caregiving at a minimun requires physicians and patients. People who are really sick go to a hospital or arrive there by ambulance, and most often receive care from physicians. It follows that changes in the acute care sector or the medical profession in the 1990s affect the delivery of emergency care in the field. The fate of hospitals and physicians between 1965 and 1982 had a direct impact on the future directions of EMS in America. On the other hand, the changes undergone by the medical profession and the acute care sector from 1870 to 1964 made the EMS revolution both possible and necessary.

EMS pioneers piggybacked on the logical and essential thrusts of movements that had combined to form the basis for a restructuring of critical care medicine. American physicians became better trained and increasingly specialized as the nineteenth century ended and the twentieth century wore on. Scientific discoveries identified vaccines for widespread communicable diseases and the general public warmed to the idea of physician specialists addressing specific types of diseases. If physicians had been regarded as charlatans as late as the time of the Spanish American War, then they were lionized as nearly omniscient scientific warriors quite capable of battling a whole host of maladies by the time World War II had erupted.

At the same time, physicians were evolving toward technocratic medicine and away from patient-centered general practice arrangements. The transition continued in the sixties, seventies, and eighties, but it did not culminate in an absolute victory for CAT Scanners over bedside manners. In the late eighties, Harvard Medical School reversed a century-old drift toward treating diseases more than patients by requiring medical students to deal with humans as humans. Clinical rotations and rounds were scheduled much earlier than was customary in their course of study. The departure was a controversial one, for it signified more changes within critical care medicine in the nineties.

The medical profession was widely trusted and admired in 1964. The seventies saw radicals castigating an evil health empire and describing physicians as nefarious villians. The tide of hostility ebbed in the eighties under Ronald Reagan, and as he took charge of Medicare among other things, physicians once again had the public's sympathy since they were cast in the roles of slaves to defensive medicine, and victims of malpractice premium overcharges and purportedly unscrupulous lawyers. The image of the physician went full circle during the period of the EMS revolution.

Technocratic medicine and increased specialization wrought profound alterations in the sixties. Physician visits to the patient's home grew scarce. Subacute medicine could be obtained in the office of a general practitioner. After a couple of years it was more likely that you would find yourself in some neighborhood-based office for a specialized group practice! EMS physicians as such were nowhere to be found in the sixties. Deadly serious medicine was the exclusive province of dedicated specialists who labored in hospitals.

Hospital-based specialty care seems to be a norm in the last decade of the twentieth century. It appears logical to us that complicated surgeries should be performed in a fairly large hospital endowed with enormously expensive diagnostic and operating room equipment, and supported either directly or indirectly by at least a dozen medical technicians of various types. Certainly, the unbridled growth of the medical specialties required the development of appropriate hospital facilities, clinics, surgicenters, and rehabilitation centers. Medicare and Medicaid funds fueled the technocratic fires in the sixties and seventies. Health planners and third party payors were finding it difficult to contain the runaway inflation afflicting health care and the acute care sector in particular. The eighties saw the cycle of seemingly limitless funds as a catalyst for hospital growth with no real bounds sputter to a halt.

Diagnosis Related Groups and Medicare Screens were measures invented by well-intentioned public health professors together with overly zealous health planners in a bid to contain hospital costs. Diagnosis Related Groups (DRGs) were perfected in New Jersey on a massive scale involving about a quarter of its hospitals. Four other eastern states pursued a much more modified approach to cost containment via DRGs. DRGs meant price fixing based on the procedures being employed. Extra efforts of any kind were effectively disallowed because the hospital could not bill for them. In fact, the DRG approach rewarded hospitals if they took short cuts—doing less and charging the fixed rate meant the facility could pocket the difference.

Care Screens were another method of containing hospital costs. They were calls from Big Brother or Big Government for case audits of the treatment given to Medicare patients. In the mid-eighties, hospital billing cycles came to be comprised by five or six quarters. Cases were held out for fuller examination before the hospital actually got paid. Advanced Life Support cases brought in by paramedics could and did get caught in the shuffle. Hospitals and ambulance systems found it harder to bill for cardiac and respiratory patients on the Cape Cod Peninsula because extensive Medicare and prospective payment schemes were being pioneered there. The entire shape of things shifted to an EMS world in which patients had to be salvaged long enough to make the screen minimum for days in the hospital, and long enough to reach outlying barriers (ceilings on charges for procedures performed within a given time period) whose maximum would take the EMS provider far past an imaginary trim point.

In theory, as the time the patient spent in the hospital became even more paramount in the nineties, one did not dare to discharge a patient prematurely, because if that same patient were to be readmitted for the identical problem in less than thirty days thereafter, the hospital could not bill the patient for the second stay in the hospital. Not surprisingly, hospitals have begun to hold patients until they are absolutely sure that they can be discharged.

Anyone familiar with the emergency care field between 1983 and 1990 can easily attest to the repercussions of this situation. Beds fill up and stay full, while physicians and nurses grow irritated with the passage of time. EMS crews trip over emergency room receiving areas crowded with ward beds and king-sized support equipment. Ambulances are diverted away from the once familiar emergency rooms—emergency rooms that are just a short ride from any point in their primary service area; instead, ambulance crews haul patients almost a half an hour in either direction. The hospital is clogged on the inside, and EMS becomes disorganized and illogical on the outside as a direct result.

The partial triumph of technocratic (or iatrocentric) medicine combined with the brief yet very intense era of hospital expansion and diversification from 1964 through 1984 forms the backdrop for the discussion that follows. The eighties were a low point for EMS for a variety of reasons. A deflated acute care sector, and an overlooked regionalized health care, which was being supplanted by networks and highly specialized care training for physicians detracted markedly from any notion of EMS as a species of public health. Was it inevitable that critical care would prove in the long run to be a millstone around the EMS provider's neck?

Couldn't the hospital extend itself into the community by various types of outreach activity? If it were a teaching hospital, with plenty of interns and the occasional resident to spare, couldn't the hospital humor idealistic people from among the academic physician ranks by allowing them to experiment with brand new methods of outreach? Mobile coronary care units staffed by physicians or physician extenders would no doubt do the trick. Mobile Coronary Care Units (MCCUs) came to be the hallmark of exhaustively trained EMTs in New Haven, of facilities in lower Manhattan, and of pilot or experimental programs in neighboring New Jersey. The paramedic oriented delivery system model was not the exclusive domain of physicians working with fire departments in California, Florida, and elsewhere. Paramedical training concepts were tested and validated at Yale and the Wharton School, too. Personnel and the refinement of skills were not the whole story. Fast-moving vehicles capable of carrying fairly sophisticated extenders of the physician's own skill, knowledge, or license were successfully put out on the street in service Belfast, UK by Dr. J. Frank Pantridge.

Dr. Pantridge evolved a marvelous fast-moving response system in the late sixties. The system was perfectly constituted for responding to cardiac emergencies within a city that came to be gripped now and then by traumas and medical emergencies stemming from a sectarian war that was four centuries old, and counting. Royal Victoria Hospital implemented the system. The seventies and eighties were to produce clones of the hospital operated extension of coronary care into the community. Oslo, Norway had this extension; Leningrad, USSR claimed to have one. But what of the Americans? What happened? Did fire surgeons beat hospital-based internists to the punch?

The answer is no. MCCU programs in countries with at least the skeletal framework for a national health system could mandate the provision of hospital-based services into the community. In America, New Jersey came closest to that type of delivery system. After very humble beginnings with a handful of volunteer-staffed paramedic demonstration projects in the mid-seventies, the state initiated hospital-based billing for mobile intensive care services. More than twenty-five units reached out to touch the needy among four million of a possible seven million New Jerseyans by 1985. The state accomplished this for a number of unique reasons.

New Jersey had several benefits: a) hospital rates were set by regulatory authorities at the state level; b) reimbursement under Medicare for paramedic physician-extending in the field was assigned as though this activity had taken place in the hospital itself; c) an enormous fleet of transport ambulances were available due to more than four decades of volunteer first aid traditions; d) a similarly large pool of variously trained volunteer EMS personnel stood ready to help; and e) a state Medical Director for EMS—a veteran of early MCCU experiments in New York City—formulated an EMS systems plan that was centered on Cardiac Resource Hospitals. In other words, Medicare paid for fly cars staffed with medics that went on to treat patients who were in turn transported in vollie rigs to an appropriate hospital. The whole thing was a hospital cost center. It worked very well for about three years. There was no reason to improve it. The Health Care Finance Administration in Baltimore questioned it in its entirety since there were no physicians in the ambulances and the fly cars were unlikely to transport patients in most cases. The Mobile Intensive Care Unit system survives in an altered yet expanded format even today, but the charges associated with it are much different. Regionalization atrophied and suffocated while the Reagan Administration's policies lent support to local, parochial, and ultimately destabilizing forces within health care.

New Jersey from 1979 through 1985 bore fruit for the DEMS regionalization effort, but the harvest came rather late. The cardiac oriented system achieved advanced life support coverage for the majority of its citizens. Dr. David R. Boyd, in a meeting at Newport, Rhode Island in October of 1980, gave New Jersey EMS people credit for piecing together a scheme that might work even though it was not rooted in Trauma, level one Trauma Centers, or the reallocation of EMS resources needed to feed one to the other. New Jersey was the exception that proved the rule.

Parochial interests and hospital market share areas stood squarely in the way of regionwide redistribution of resources and the attendant redirection of patient flow. The reordering of the hospital world, whether at the behest of Regional Medical Programs (RMPs), Robert Wood Johnson Foundation, or the Division of Emergency Medical Services, was and still is largely impossible. Expansion fueled by Medicare, Medicaid, Blue Cross and Blue Shield, and most private payors did not fit in well with the kind of awe inspiring redistricting that Dr. Boyd and others like him had proposed.

In truth, as many saw it, EMS dealt with either cardiacs or traumas. Some additional last minute postscripts were assigned to burns and poisonings. Cardiacs were part of the focus of the earliest EMS legislation in the sixties. Traumas—or injuries leading to accidental deaths—were the principal focus of that legislation (see Chapters 7–10). Despite tremendous strides toward better prehospital emergency cardiac care in unique areas such as Seattle (see Chapter 11), and without negating the considerable impact of Citizen CPR on EMS outreach, it is fair to say that cardiac care in the prehospital environment between 1964 and the present has been a difficult uphill struggle. Even today, heart blockers are being tried on an experimental basis while state level EMS authorities consider incorporating defibrillation—smart or otherwise—into basic EMT curricula. For much of the sixties and the seventies, cardiacs were treated by physicians working in hospitals. When was the first paramedic class held in New York City? Did most Americans have prehospital ALS available to them before 1980? When advanced life support systems were created, due to Robert Wood Johnson, or DEMS, or local initiative, they were often geared toward treatment of lethal arrhythmias. Traumas, on the other hand, seemed to require BLS skills.

Department of Transportation personnel working from a highway safety orientation found the war against accidental death to be comprised of an earnest effort to situate EMS personnel capable of gathering up the squash traumas on the nation's highways. They also emphasized safety and prevention measures such as "drinking while intoxicated" legislation, seat belt laws, and reduction in state speed limits. Robert Wood Johnson echoed the response system aspects of this orientation. DEMS spawned trauma research, and required the implementation of regional trauma centers in the last two years of a seven year campaign.

Cardiac EMS and trauma EMS were historically different, and were engulfed by much different circumstances. Random differences, such as those between internal medicine and surgery, did not have to lead to separate systems, distinct legacies, or worse yet, confusion. Nothing shatters dogmatic certitude more than confusion.

Race, sex, age, climate, culture, and geographic area can all help determine how many traumas versus how many cardiacs the EMS providers will treat in the course of a year, three years, or five years in any particular region of the country. Resident trauma physicians would find it difficult to hone their skills in North Dakota. Cardiologists and internists might be much more likely to prosper in an urban environment. Rural EMS and urban EMS both have their difficulties due to different circumstances, but rural EMS seems to be the harder of the two.

The demand for EMS and critical care medicine far surpasses the supply in New York City, Philadelphia, Washington, DC, Newark, New Jersey, and so on. Rural EMS is low volume, urban EMS is high volume, and critical care medicine comes into play in both instances. Long ago, in theory, there was a regional plan for just about any of 304 EMS regions in which specialty centers could be designated and in which resources were configured to address the known or predicted need for patients of that type. The trouble was that somebody had to sell the concept to a wide audience—an audience that included the general public.

CHAPTER SIX

——— ✳ ———

Witnessing

There is nobody so happy as the person cast in the role of a preacher to those who are already among the converted. Religious ardor, personal fervor, and just a pinch of cant are all part of a recipe for a laying on of hands, exorcising demons, or performing a really terrific rock concert. EMS extravaganzas at the national level circa 1990 can and do become mired in the clinical equivalent of sound bytes. Speakers are paid tidy sums to provide what is commonly known on the lecture circuit as **info-tainment**. Conveying information is scarcely the goal. Entertainment or small scale theatricals overflowing with beautiful slides or media-hyped custom movies suffice to fill the bill. The audience pays good money and it is therefore entitled to a circus.

Sadly, two types of EMS megaconference attendees rear their ugly heads and try to spoil things. Bantering of one sort or another was not at all uncommon back in the seventies when Dr. Boyd and his followers were trying to impress one and all with clear and shining dogmas. Now a resurgence of these ideologies has begun in the nineties. It is almost enough to restore one's faith in the EMS movement! The first type of EMS rebel is the young, idealistic, and naive EMS provider clinging to the true faith. Type I providers think the individual is still important. They are sure that EMS is both possible and sacred. Seasoned info-tainment circuit riders dismiss

them as simpletons. To them, emotion has no place in an organized, if less than well established, religion.

The second type of upstart EMS provider is the serious concert-
goer. Type II individuals have about 2.5 academic degrees. They are
usually either paramedics or BSN level nurses. They consider EMS
to be a serious business. You might find their sort running steward-
ship campaigns among high church Presbyterian congregations in
the upper South. These deadly serious folks have the temerity to
demand the functional equivalent of graduate school public health
or public administration seminar. And they do so without any expectation of a patch, a many-colored badge for their lapel, or the
minimum of two additional wallet cards! They do not require a
neon tee shirt with the show's name on it for their personal use on
the beach. Zealots and plan-making experts are just no fun. Who
ever said EMS needed both a heart and a mind?

In 1964, a number of people were beginning to think about
communications. Upper middle class, discontent with the Eisenhower
era, evolved into a more nearly anarchistic mode of expression in
the early sixties. A motto was: Morality is absolute, but ethics are
situational. Relativism was supposedly liberating—more so than bon-
gos in the fifties. Modern authors like J. D. Salinger displaced
earlier existentialist opponents of totalitarianism like George Orwell
in their affections. More surprisingly, a longshoreman with an eighth
grade education became the philospher king of the ambivalent
liberal intelligentsia. Television commentators and literary critics
alike celebrated Eric Hoffer as the poor man's answer to Plato,
Hedonism, or the syspeak (systems' speak) pouring out of America's
MBA programs.

As the ultraleft grew beyond being rebels without a cause,
opting instead for rejecting the absurdity of maturing in order to
emerge as people possessed of a single dimension, most Americans
used the television as a palliative, a babysitter, or an excuse to avoid
divorce court. The ultraright grew beyond being people with ulcers
going down for the count in a neat grey suit, choosing instead a
technocratic mindset which hypnotized them into believing that
Indonesia, the Dominican Republic, and Vietnam were good opportunities to make up for the shameful failure to win the Korean
War. Many Americans did not take much note of increasingly ambitious military adventures because in between family situation com-

edies, formula westerns, formula detective shows, and sterling physician models, we always seemed to be winning World War II. Critics began to complain about sixties television.

Television was wasteful and in large measure insidious. It had the power to assume an undue influence over our lives. The messages being imparted were somehow swallowed up by the electronic messenger itself. Television was something of a god.

Scholars argued that television was destined to become the foremost shaper of the American mind. They would not have been taken aback by the spectacle of three cable network reporters based in Iraq broadcasting the actual outbreak of a major war from a hostile capital in January of 1991. The idea was to make history and then tell everyone about the story line that broadcasting played a major role in creating.

Media analysts and radical thinkers of previous generations had foreseen the dementia associated with a big lie that is repeated over and over again. They had shouted at it in the thirties—and did so from Baton Rouge to Berlin. After World War II, the Madison Avenue mentality celebrated the artistry of subliminal suggestions—short cuts or bytes of an image revolving around a particular product or product line. The triumph of this type of media presentation continued through the fifties and right on into the sixties.

The sixties presented more of a challenge. It was to become a decade of skepticism. "Liberal Great Society" concepts faded from view as a large minority of Americans sought an honorable peace and left the fate of the elderly to a trickle down theory of economic development—old folks who were ashamed of food stamps could always buy dog food at the grocery store. Major corporations were widely hated by radicals and radicalized liberals alike. After all, the people who made your lunch leftovers stay fresh also made one of the nastiest bombs available anywhere. And the evening news gave avid testaments to its effects!

The seventies saw televised impeachment proceedings begin against President Nixon. Media people claimed with some justification that they had in effect become a fourth branch of the American Government—they had restrained an evil executive branch by investigating its excesses. Two newspaper reporters found themselves depicted by Dustin Hoffman and Robert Redford in the movie that followed. Television tried to preserve liberal values in the shows it offered to people living in a country that had somehow or other, for all intents and purposes, lost the war. It was also a country plagued by recessions, and presided over for a time by a man who hadn't even been elected President. The man who finished the decade was long on human rights but much longer still on fiscal conservatism. The media mirrored a country prone to soul searching and devoid of the aggressive exhuberance of the early sixties. American hostages appeared on the screen as their Iranian captors paraded them down the streets of Teheran. The country seemed almost impotent.

In the eighties, Americans lurched forward, away from self-doubt and self-pity, settling happily for the consummate media politician. A movie actor gave the majority of Americans a new sense of pride as he strengthened the defense establishment. He most emphatically did not similarly reconstitute social or health care programs (e.g., Title 12-EMSS Act). He did build up law enforcement and related community programs (e.g., NHTSA—injury control and accident prevention). The term "federal" came to be an anachronism. "Liberal" would be a term that was largely unknown to people in their twenties, as they voted for George Bush against a relic of the bad old days named Michael Dukakis.

Reagan was at home on television. His political enemies compared him to a teflon pan—nothing bad ever stuck to him. A decade later his radical daughter accused him of creating the homeless problem by cutting the funding for mental health facilities and causing the patients to be dumped out on the streets. It was not exactly a big news story. His wife's tell-all book did not stick to him either. EMS advocates like to relate how a trauma center saved the Gipper as he exsanguinated on the ER floor, only to have him eliminate monies for trauma centers less than a year later. The image did not make a lasting impression on a lot of EMS supporters.

Popular images on television screens of the previous decade paved the way for Reagan's frank dismissal of social and health care agendas—sometimes losing a baby or two along with the bath. "Effete," "whimpering," "wasteful," and "unable to act" were the key words used to reject Big Government and the liberal people responsible for building it. The quality of domestic life would be diminished while the nation's security was given a much needed upgrade—an upgrade that made people feel better until the television brought back the familiar notion of impotence in a place called Beirut. Certainly, a few things that were worth keeping got lost in the "no government equals good government" shuffle. Standardized and regionalized EMS was one of them.

The loss of good things was not noticed at first because revenge on the Democrat superbureaucracy of the thirties, forties, fifties, and sixties was more important. The government abandoned its responsibilities in EMS and many other fields. Deregulation and decentralization went hand in hand. At the White House, they pulled the plug on the airline industry, banking industry, and EMS system. The states could and would handle it; some people cheered.

Many EMS advocates cheered, too. The end of ruinous interference at the national level was at hand. EMS was free to grow to maturity at the local level. Nobody from Washington, DC would come to stir things up any longer. Dangerous ideas like regional specialty centers and national standards no longer stood in the way of parochial or myopic perspectives on the way EMS should operate.

The climate of opinion in 1983 was somewhat different depending on where you looked. Local concerns took precedence over state or national concerns. Deregulation meant dog-eat-dog competition for pricing of airline flights, savings and loan investment practices, and the planning of emergency care response systems. Conservatives called it "freedom." Moderates called it "enlightened" bordering on "reckless." Radical social theorists dismissed it as Fascist. It is fair to say that decentralizing the social and health care programs of the previous fifty years had the potential to create vacuums.

If less than half of the states had Level I trauma centers, then who would make the recalcitrant states do something about their refusal to grasp the supposed state-of-the-art system (see Chapters 9 and 10)? If a trauma patient had ten things wrong with her, and you could only hope to group the four most lucrative problems in the bill sent to her insurance company, then where would your hospital turn to obtain the remaining charges for the six you had to leave off the bill? When you group together charges to offset expected losses, and you determine that regionalized specialty care can sometimes lead to cost shifting within once stable hospitals, then is health care actually anything close to fee-for-service at that point? Communicating is rather difficult when words lose their old meanings.

Semantics seem for all the world to be some kind of a dodge—an academic or artistic retreat from a straight and narrow bottom line. But EMS from 1964 through today has been the victim rather than the beneficiary of failures to communicate. EMS people promise as much or more than the dinosaur liberals of LBJ's day. EMS saves lives. EMS saves lives! EMS saves lives?

Emergency care personnel have been offering EMS as a panacea to many types of horrible episodes in the normal person's world. EMS has a long and venerable tradition of proselytizing for itself. The impact of this effort to help Americans let EMS help them has been stunning, frightening, and for the most part rather ephemeral. It is trite to dismiss all of EMS for twenty-six years—years that nevertheless amount to a signal failure to get a clear message across. On the one hand, organized and comprehensive EMS systems did not emerge until the late sixties at the earliest. On the other hand, there was, is, and probably always will be more than one message.

IN THE BEGINNING

A physician wrote a popular article in a popular magazine to point out that cardiac death was suddenly all the rage. Teams of scientists announced that accidental death and disability were way out of hand. A new federal agency started the proliferation of materials marked with a green cross. Driver education classes at certain high schools received better, although more disturbing, movies to watch. A popular movie portrayed the ambulance business as a bittersweet exercise in soul-searching, while casting as much sand as possible against the tide.

A BIT LATER

The cardiac side of the house offered Citizen CPR. People who recalled a show called "Rescue 8" were suddenly made aware of telemetry, physician extension by paramedics, and the nuances of rescue portrayed by a long-running show called "Emergency." The trauma side of the house at least had equal footing at the first of many EMS training standards conferences in 1969. A second national level conference in 1971 continued a snowball effect that led to the inclusion of a program for accidental death in Richard Nixon's list of important problems confronting the nation, as he prepared to begin the quest for another term in the Oval Office.

STILL LATER

Shortly after Nixon's untimely departure, and in the wake of the advent of David R. Boyd, MDCM as the Director of a public health service EMS effort, Americans were at times exposed to EMS people. Dr. Boyd earnestly believed that public information and education was almost as important as scientific research in advancing the concept of systematic emergency care. Not only did federal officials preach to EMS grant staff at conferences held in ten federal regions throughout the country (and these conferences were swollen by attendees who were cynical and frightened as they pursued the gold behind the golden rule), the attendees themselves were expected to return to the 304 lesser regions and spread the good word. Dr. Boyd himself was a prime example. He posed with governors, senators, and local television newscasters. A spinoff was a short-lived EMS educational television network in California. Dr. Boyd went on the "Phil Donahue Show" when the American College of Emergency Practice became much more formally recognized as a legitimate specialty.

Local area populations were to be made aware of EMS as Dr. Boyd himself increased the awareness of many EMS people and television watchers. The primary weapons were newsletters, public service announcements, and high profile activities. You could attract a great deal of attention by filling a football stadium with CPR students. There were dividends to be harvested, in the short run.

AND STILL LATER

EMS on a regional basis required a huge leap of faith. You went ahead and promised a wide variety of people that a system would: 1) exist; 2) make a tangible difference in reducing unnecessary deaths in just three short years; and 3) progress to a more definitive level of advanced care, for a greater impact on the problem of unnecessary death. So many promises to keep! From 1974 through 1982, Boyd's regions made these dramatic claims to a country bewildered by a peace with honor, a presidential pardon, a recession, the mystic invocation of human rights, tormented hostages in Iran, and a White House budget director prone to creating deficits for social programs as a logical prerequisite to eliminating them. Just what was the actual state-of-the-art for physician-directed paramedics in 1980? How many regions could reasonably aspire to deliver advanced life support in 1980? Did organized EMS reach a point of diminishing returns where emergency care merely changed the place and the time of the patient's death? How many cardiac emergencies treated by EMS lived long enough to be discharged alive from the hospital in 1990—a simple majority? Promises led to expectations.

EMS people inspired by public health service bore witness to a miracle. When DEMS faded from view in 1982, the American Heart Association, the American Red Cross, the National Highway Traffic Safety Administration, and ACEP kept the spirit alive with public service announcements that broadcast more specific, and a bit more modest, promises.

FADING TO THE BACKGROUND

Television in the eighties offered a show called "Trauma Center," which ran for less than a year. A made-for-television movie celebrated Dr. R. Adams Cowley and his career in Maryland. It featured actor William Conrad, who provided the narration for the mythical Dr. Kimble two decades earlier. It is not listed in any video guide currently available. A comedy entitled "ER" about an emergency room doctor (Elliot Gould) faired little better. A liberal-left holdover about a hospital in Boston ("Saint Elsewhere") featured a janitor turned paramedic. The emergency room doctor, played by Howie Mandel, was strange, but today the actor is a high-profile comedian.

As the last decade of the twentieth century began, television rediscovered the search and rescue side of police work and fire suppression. EMS made it into these shows through the back door— a door that equates paramedics with police or fire personnel. A movie portrayed paramedics in a farcical manner, making them analogous to a long series of figures seen in several police farces popular in the late eighties, such as *Police Academy* and *The Paramedics.*

Did EMS actually travel from the status of a notable if noisy crusade to that of a caricature in popular film, or that of the backside of rescue work? Do trauma centers evoke the image of the miracle-producing height of specialty care medicine today? Or are they shameful drains through which countless dollars pour? Are drug dealers deserving of $186,000 worth of care, considering the fact that they have no known source of health insurance?

In the past few years, Dr. Donald Trunkey, who works in Oregon, and Dr. Howard Champion, a very famous surgeon and researcher working in Washington, DC, have been asked to defend the concept of one trauma-EMS system for everyone—both rich and poor alike. Their arguments in favor of it hark back to the storied idealism of the seventies. The audiences remain skeptical, if not hostile, and Congress is one of these audiences.

Witnessing is an essential part of building something new and exciting. Sometimes you have to make your point before you can actually hope to prove your point. EMS had to convince the myriad powers that be. The message varied slightly from place to place: "EMS saves lives," "a system to save a life," "the system is the solution," "EMTs do it on the road," "EMTs only respond to you," "Every Marriage Suffers," "over eight million saved," etc. From 1964 to 1990, many tribes announced that EMS had arrived. Promises were made. A remarkable number of them were kept; but there were too many voices offering them! It was hard to distinguish who was involved.

Was EMS part of public safety and therefore a logical extension of the rescue side of fire department work? Could the police do it instead? Was a third service the ideal solution—a solution that would put EMS on an equal footing with the other two? Was the hospital a viable operating agency? Was EMS pretty much public health—falling under the heading of community and preventive medicine? Was Dr. Boyd the medical director of a national emergency medical services system? Or was EMS a type of public safety somehow connected to the prevention of accidental deaths on the highway and in the home? If so, shouldn't the National Highway Traffic Safety Administration be the main center of direction from

Washington, DC? Was cardiac death something that EMS could really address with advanced life support? Was traumatic injury or death a more realistic target for systematic emergency care?

So many voices raised in seldomly fruitful efforts to get someone's attention! The next four chapters of this book examine four of the loudest voices in the EMS chorus. Each is important in its own right. No one of them has an exclusive claim to truth.

CHAPTER SEVEN

———— ✳ ————

Public Health—EMS as Acute Care, Ambulatory Care, or Primary Care

Emergency Medical Services have an impact on the communities they serve. It is not stretching a point to suggest that EMS really ought to have a significant effect on the public's health. After all, the reduction of mortality due to heart attacks is an important result of EMS. A clear reduction in the morbidity stemming from multiple (squash) traumas is also an important result of EMS. Both results would have to be considered genuine contributions to the overall health status of any community. EMS can save lives—sometimes! EMS can minimize the lasting damage associated with accidental injuries—sometimes. Researchers and more than a few bureaucrats proudly proclaim that EMS returns years of life lost to the American economy. Labor is returned to the tune of $21,000 per year for each year that the salvaged patient manages to keep contributing to: the work force; the purchasing power of the work force; the productivity of the work force; and the stability of a regional economy.

If EMS returns a twenty-six year old female systems analyst to a full and active life after a major automobile accident, and she goes on to work for another twenty years, then EMS protected at least $420,000 worth of action for the grocers, car dealers, hairdressers, and of course, the U.S. Internal Revenue Service. If she is a rather talented systems analyst, then she might go on to double her income and yield a cool million in return for EMS's prowess early on in her life. EMS is good for business, and it is certainly good for the hospital business—most of the time.

Is EMS just as good for the community-based ambulatory care center or the "Doc-in-the-Box" business? Does the local freestanding emergicenter or urgicenter benefit from EMS traditions? And how do these centers interface with the area hospitals' emergency rooms? The answers to such questions follow from one essential fact of life between 1973 and 1990: EMS had to change in order to maintain and expand its place in the health care delivery system.

The system can be loosely defined as one in which the population's health status and overall well-being are analyzed with a view toward making everyone fairly comfortable with their own individual health status. The miracle cure and the hospice compete for position in contemporary public health thinking. Helping an AIDS patient on the verge of suicide feel comfortable and dignified might fill the bill for certain radical thinkers. Rationalizing the remaining moments of a once bouyant cancer patient might signify an accomplishment for other radicals, such as those who hate the living will for religious reasons. Where does that leave EMS? The art of causing the patient to accept his or her fate is an elusive skill to maintain in an EMS environment.

EMS providers in the street or in the hospital environment often deal with emergency situations. These situations demand an adjustment reaction on the part of the patient, or those closely associated with the patient, and by the personnel rendering first aid or delivering emergency care to that patient. Bringing about a calm reaction that borders on acceptance in an emergent patient is next to impossible. EMS folks have a relatively short amount of time to combat legitimate fears and intense denial on the part of the individual patient. If present-day emergency care delivery systems have to encounter this type of difficulty in the process of trying to make their patients feel comfortable about the sudden alterations Fate has wrought in their once peaceful lives, then the non-systems of 1964 had almost no chance of doing so at all.

The scattered elements of what would soon combine to form a vigorous new addition to the acute care sector medicine, and a source of unexpected sustenance for the little-known fields of ambulatory care and primary care, were hard to recognize at that point in time. Young people were more interested in surfing, while their World War II era parents were looking to shower their offspring with possessions—something the elder generation had always lacked during the depression of the thirties. If somebody cracked up the hot rod, or fell after drinking too much at a party, then the 1964 state-of-the-art awaited them.

Imagine this disturbing scenario: untrained attendants running hearses to and from emergency rooms that were staffed by physicians assigned there against their will. It was reasonably typical of many locales prior to the onset of brazen schemes and even more brazen people bent on nothing less than a revolution in emergency care. EMS in 1964 was virgin ground for those clamoring to be innovative.

Clearly, as was discussed earlier (see Chapter 5), EMS could operate out of the emergency department(s) of one or more hospitals. It was attempted in the Northeast and the Midwest. It was honed to a fine art for nearly two decades in Georgia, where ambulance attendants came to have an in-hospital cost center to defray the costs of operating EMS in the more rural areas of that state. Hospitals could buy or lease ambulances in order to improve their outreach into the community, and feather their own nests with at least some of the patients. Acute care sector economics demanded an edge against competing hospitals. Ambulance services were and still are something of a competitive advantage. Upgrading the hospital itself was even more of an advantage, and EMS provided the basis for doing so from 1973 to 1982.

EMS resource hospitals achieved a great deal of prestige, and through it a greater overall market share during the heyday of Dr. Boyd's systemization effort. Individual hospitals could and did make conspicuous efforts to regionalize medical control and patient placement patterns under the guise of better lifesaving care for cardiacs, traumas, burns, spinal cord injuries, high risk infants, poisonings, drug and alcohol related problems, and behavioral emergencies. Cardiac resource hospitals bought into the most lucrative proposition—the patients generated large bills and were generally insured. Trauma resource hospitals often signed off on what would become, by 1986, their own economic death warrants. Pediatric trauma centers did a bit better because of a tendency by other hospitals to transfer or sometimes shunt complicated pediatric traumas into a more definitive level of care. The economics of EMS were more than a little complicated from 1973 through 1986.

Hospitals gained a short term market advantage by resourcing Dr. Boyd's systematic approach to critically emergent patients. When Dr. Boyd's DEMS fell from grace in 1982, and decentralization of most federal health planning agencies gained the upper hand, many of these same hospitals found that their golden aura was quickly eroding.

Plain and simple EMS is easier to sustain. A useful rule of thumb from the early seventies on would be that *thirty percent of all patients taken to a given hospital's emergency room wound up being admits to the hospital itself.* With or without an ambulance service, the hospital was fed a steady diet of one type or another by its very own emergency department. EMS generates business; EMS means a predictable source of in-house referrals.

By extension, it can be argued that seventy percent of the patients seen in the emergency room use the outpatient side of the curtain as a *de facto* neighborhood health clinic. In the seventies, health planners and some EMS administrators complained about this situation by decrying bogus utilization. Some enlightened emergency care physicians saw in all of this a golden opportunity that didn't come from Washington, DC. If the outpatient side of emergency rooms were being sorely taxed, then this surely meant there was an untapped market out in the American population. Many Americans had a need for less than acute care. Some Americans, generally either the middle class or those who were poor but who were also covered by the surviving elements of liberal entitlement programs (e.g., Medicaid, WIC), were in a position to demand this type of care because they could pay for it.

EMS went suburban; it went beyond the knife and gun club or still fashionable heart attacks to embrace insurance physicals, workman's compensation cases, rehabilitation needs, and permanent eyeliner in multiple colors, featuring both surgical and cosmetological consultants. The freestanding emergency care concept rose like a soaring phoenix out of the ashes of a failed national initiative geared toward organizing and constituting all emergency care. The Aesculapian star decorated the wondrously paneled suites of EMS physicians gone suburban—so suburban that their patrons were spared the grotesque ugliness of sitting in a busy emergency room holding area for a number of hours. The names outside the suites were eventually changed to freestanding ambulatory care centers by the late eighties. Malpractice premiums afforded group rates for a certain maximum level of out-of-hospital care—care that could not go beyond of the hospital setting. Emergency was an advertisement for around-the-clock physician staffing. Freestanding ambulatory care was not.

It is very hard to imagine just how significant suburban EMS was, is, and, no doubt, will be in the future. In the seventies, family practice physicians meeting in Denver and elsewhere tried to reestablish the concept of the general practice and patient oriented physician. They wanted to fill a perceived gap in the American health care market. The scheme has yet to catch on in a large scale way.

In the last twelve years, the EMS physician working in the freestanding ambulatory care environment has been instrumental in plugging that gap. Suburban patients living in residential areas, where houses turnover every three years due to corporate relocations, find solace in a clearly marked Freestanding Ambulatory Care Center (FAC) that often accepts credit cards. The eight-hour wait of the hospital emergency room is shortened to as few as twenty minutes before the patient gives a full history, has vitals taken, sits listening to Muzak, and is further comforted by yellow walls in a climate controlled examination room. The family doctor can be readily supplanted by the EMS physician.

EMS is a branch of health care that begins with high risk infants and ends with courtesy transports to the home or to the hospice for elderly patients leaving skilled nursing homes. EMS people from EMT all the way up to diplomate physician know more than a little bit about a whole bunch of distinct classes of presenting symptoms. From babies to the elderly, EMS covers a very wide spectrum of care. The demands and unmet needs are enormous. The intensity and the acuity that animate a high level examination in an FAC or in the outpatient department side of a hospital's emergency receiving area are as taxing as some of the ten most common surgical procedures. The remnants of the reimbursement authorities at the federal level have recognized this fact. They have implemented measures calculated to give EMS-FAC-OPD patient assessments a higher reimbursement level than several of the top ten—most popular or frequently chosen—surgical operations. Screening a feverish adolescent female can be more intensive than a bowel resection. A high level workup on a severe case of venereal disease generates more charges than the hands of the gods at play on a damaged gastrointestinal tract.

EMS caregiving in the eighties and nineties is a far cry from the pure resourcing of specialty care that characterized the late sixties and all of the seventies. EMS physicians can drop the bravado illusion of tireless surgical skill and medical ardor after a successful residency and put their name on a group shingle in order to render very fine ambulatory care. Annual physicals and discreet probing after dietary habits, seeming psychological problems, or unfortunate problems such as smoking or drinking to excess all border on primary care. In the seventies, an alcoholic might have stumbled, and thereby sustained blunt traumatic injuries to the head and upper extremeties. The emergency room physician might have assessed the immediate status of the patient and then gone on to identify additional areas for concern located in the lower extremeties. Unattended gangrene would be detected because a drunken person fell down and somehow found their way to a hospital ER. Today, the FAC effectively screens patients, too.

The patient, rather than the injury or the disease, is the focus of the treatment plan. Health care is patient-driven, and the EMS physician working in the FAC environment must strive to meet the individual patient's needs. If you go into the FAC for a small but painful laceration, then you might well find yourself being put on a diet to control blood pressure problems born of a clear tendency toward obesity.

Sadly, EMTs and paramedics do not work in the FAC as much as physicians or nurses. They do have meaningful opportunities in the fields of after care or home health. They can teach first aid or CPR to the greater public. EMS personnel can bear witness to the importance of diet, the merits of wearing seat belts, the importance of the safe storage of medicines and household chemicals, and, some might say, the need for gun control.

EMS providers see a number of sickening, annoying, and altogether stupid things that affect the health status and well-being of certain members of the general public. Injury control was a pet peeve of EMS pioneers as early as 1965. It remains an important facet of the American Public Health Association in the 1990s. Primary care aims at maintaining wellness. It also employs myopic pedants who graduate from what many term Schools of Public Disease. Preventive medicine entails work from the American Heart Association, the American Red Cross, the American Trauma Society, the National Safety Council, ACEP and their EMS oriented surgical counterparts, CPR instructors, many paramedics, some EMTs, and perhaps a few first responders.

EMS diversified itself insofar as hospitals and emergency rooms were concerned from the mid-seventies onward. The migration of EMS to the suburbs followed a pattern set by the rest of American society during that period. Urban blight continued unabated in most of the cities that the exiles had left behind. Some gentrification took place in Boston, Baltimore, Philadelphia, and elsewhere— ghetto housing and old warehouses were bought up for a pittance and resurrected as condos for yuppies, instantly converting squalor into fashion. It was the real estate development equivalent of swimming against the tide.

It did not translate into a reversal of the prevailing tide. By the mid-eighties, decay and exodus to the ever more distant suburbs was easy to discern in New York, Washington, DC, Los Angeles, and smaller places like Camden, New Jersey. The demands for health care issuing from the decaying cities was enormous. Guns and drugs made for huge increments in the demand for EMS personnel dedicating themselves to the management of penetrating traumas.

EMS has marked out a unique place for itself in what passes for a health care delivery system. EMS assets tend to decline in value while liabilities tend to accrue. An ambulance is depreciated over five years. A continuing year-to-date total of bad debt, uncompensated care, and uncollectables are rung up. The gaps in revenue make life miserable for the ER and the ambulance company alike. The gap is particularly acute in major cities because the demand for emergency care services, both urgent and ambulatory, far exceeds the present supply of these same services. EMS saves lives, or at least impacts positively on them, if and when it has a chance to get to the potential patient.

The need for health care (doc-in-the-boxes, OPD clinics, insurance physicals, trauma centers, etc.) is no doubt greater than the unmet and impossible to meet demand for it. This gloomy prognosis must also be applied to all of the integral facets of EMS as they are seen in the context of the overall health care delivery system.

Should there be television advertisements about the early signs of heart disease? Or should someone construct a huge chain of OPDs to serve as clinics in each and every neighborhood? Or should someone else blanket the nation with physician assistants and nurse-paramedics thereby forming the rubric of a public health service? These remedies sound fine, but who would want to pay for them?

Global and far reaching solutions were tried at the macro and micro levels in the seventies. On balance, almost all of these solutions worked; however, it was not good enough. Local customs were affected adversely. The one-shot approach to EMS went down in flames in 1982 (see Chapter 9). Diversification, reorganization, disintegration, and fragmentation have been the hallmarks of public health oriented EMS during the rest of the eighties. As we have seen, in certain locales EMS can be equated with family care medicine. EMS has other roots—roots with little or no direct connection to health care delivery systems.

CHAPTER EIGHT

───── ✳ ─────

Public Safety—EMS as the First, Second, or Third Service

Americans do not devote much time or thought to public health, or, for that matter, to emergency medical services. The nation has been organized around laws—laws that have governed the American people, with a few conspicuous exceptions, for the better part of two centuries. Through the implementation of laws, chaos is averted. Clear precedents for future action are laid down in huge tomes that chronicle America's progress toward a living tradition of case-made law. The entire corpus of legal writings give the country structure, and purportedly keep all people equal.

The biggest failure of the legal system was the Civil War, which lasted from 1861 through 1865, and resulted in the loss of more lives than all other American wars put together. Europeans and people from the Middle East are fond of chiding Americans for possessing a long military tradition, while being strangely unaccustomed to the ravages of war. Americans have never had their cities bombed, as happened in Europe during World War II. These critics would profit from a visit to Fredericksburg, Vicksburg, or Gettysburg. They might also do well to speak with people who come from a long line of once glorious rebels still actively engaged in trying to live down the psychological impact of Sherman's March to the Sea. In the 1860s, America witnessed both the devastation and the subsequent rebuilding of some of its major cities. Atlanta is quite a place now. Imagine what it might have been if it had escaped destruction at the hands of Union troops!

Americans from the north and south discovered that an overriding structure had very real virtues associated with it. A few radicals during the depression of the 1930s tried to initiate class warfare, but they failed because their best ideas were absorbed into the existing system. In the spring of 1970, a new generation of student radicals gave widespread leftist upheaval a try—a try occasioned by Ohio National Guard troops shooting and fatally wounding anti-(Vietnam) war demonstrators at Kent University in the northern part of Ohio. "Can do" Americans were in the process of losing their misguided or mistaken belief in a Madison Avenue hyped and glitzy version of the American dream. Only a few of them were willing to bomb banks, kidnap an industrialist's daughter, or destroy a university library to express their disillusionment with the prevailing order. The hideousness of the first civil war served to remind Americans that under almost all circumstances there was no rational justification for a second one.

The first civil war has more than a little significance for the later development of Emergency Medical Services. The conflict featured the extensive use of ambulances staffed by the functional equivalent of medics, and the proliferation in the North of private health care foundations staffed by volunteer women—women who singlehandedly improved camp and hospital sanitation practices on the various fronts or within the confines of hospital ships. It also featured the development, in turn, of sterile techniques by southern women staffing hospitals—the most notable of which was in Richmond, Virginia, and it also set the federal government down as the lasting arbitor of subsequent disputes in the country. As a direct result of the war, the U.S. Supreme Court and the executive branch of government soared into prominent roles in American political life. By the early part of the twentieth century, America in the final analysis was one country governed by one set of laws.

These laws were of little avail to disenfranchised African Americans from the 1890s until 1954 and then well into the sixties. These laws seemingly ignored the plight of rural Americans during the same period. The farmers tried to organize themselves into an effective political force as the rest of the country became ever more industrialized and citified. The radical farmers known as Populists, living on the farms of Georgia and Iowa, had much in common with African Americans in and around Tuskegee, Alabama in the 1890s. Both groups were subtracted out of the mainstream of American life. Although their great-grandchildren have fared much better, their situation poses unusual problems for EMS folks in the 1990s (see Chapter 12).

Francophone jurists in Louisiana are nonetheless bound by the same national standards as their distinct compatriots in Maine or Iowa. Since standards usually revolve around the protection of life and property, America after the Civil War was very much in need of insurance. It was almost unthinkable to make a move in any direction at all without it. *Ad hoc* arrangements for maintaining order and minimizing the danger to private and community property were no longer sufficient. Police departments, fire departments, and municipal authorities capable of planning for disasters were vital foundations of an increasingly urbanized and still more industrialized nation. Order, property, and foresight led to the preservation of life and the protection of property. The city official who planned for the great San Francisco earthquake was one of its most brilliant casualties. The idea of a police force going on strike became an anathema shortly after World War I. Fire service cutbacks provoke such popular resistance and outcry that you might feel a church, a synagogue, or a mosque was being wrenched from a two hundred-year-old town.

The context for the delivery of emergency care through the whole or partial auspices of public safety agencies was pretty much established during the nineteenth century. An injured or very sick patient constituted a threat of sorts to the public order and to private property. How calm was the average citizen in the face of small pox? How many tuberculosis sanitoriums were located in the middle of a thriving business district of a major town? In the 1990s, would anyone move into a neighborhood plagued by penetrating traumas that are derived from random acts of violence? Does anyone want their kids to duck bullets on the way home from school?

Police officials could obviate the need for public health concern about the threats posed by either of these cases. Water companies and fire departments routinely join forces to reduce the rate of burn deaths from household accidents, and to combat the frightful morbidity that frequently accompanies scalding in pediatric patients. The distinction between public safety and public health is not firmly drawn or harsh; partnership is implied. Sound public safety can facilitate good public health by increasing the overall safety, and with it the sense of well-being of the average citizen. But it doesn't have to do so! The public health end of the equation can reflect a bit of a tradeoff! Good public health can reduce unhealthy practices such as smoking, substance abuse, self-abuse, including varieties that lead directly to AIDS and the further spread of AIDS, child abuse, improper diet, and many forms of violent or destructive anti-social behavior. Consider the following putative maxim: healthy people are somewhat mentally healthy as well; therefore, it might be hoped that they are less prone to commit arson or murder. Now if healthy and orderly people were to multiply as a direct result of public safety and public health working together, and patient care became patient-driven in many respects, then what would EMS people be doing? The answer is "plenty" (see Chapter 12).

Unfortunately, EMS people do not have the problem of being less needed by a storybook world—a world grossly simplified by the fact that public health and public safety work together in concert. Cooperation is less apparent out in the field. Medical control of fire department EMS differs from that imposed by hospital-based physicians. Telemetry is fraught with difficulties in either event. Public safety is public safety. Public health is public health. So which one is EMS?

What is the function of EMS? During this century, maintaining order comes from the police or, at the worst, the National Guard or the Army. In newsreels from the thirties, the viewer sees soldiers in the vicinity of the White House dispersing starving veterans who are demanding a pension. Two decades later, National Guard soldiers deliver African American students to a high school in Arkansas. Federal police officers combine with the threat of federal troops to inflict a similar amount of social change on the University of Alabama and the University of Mississippi in the early sixties. Troops restored order at Kent University at the beginning of the seventies. Troops and police had reestablished order during the riots that proclaimed the death of the Great Society in the late sixties. President Nixon's running mate ran on a platform of law and order in a "can do" America that was hurting because it seemed to lack both.

The man, the heat, Dick Tracy, and maybe even Joe Friday were images associated with keeping the lid on. Police could secure the scene, and some became paramedics later on in the eighties. Police did not have to chase after escaped lepers, and did not have to put an armed guard in front of a contaminated restaurant. Order may be a prerequisite for the delivery of emergency health care under certain circumstances. Order in and of itself is not a precondition of delivering health care. In the 1990s, EMS is done under dubious conditions in a frankly unhealthy environment (see Chapter 12).

Police personnel are unlike EMS personnel in one respect— police personnel do not get paid directly by their rate of arrests made per pay period. There is no fixed monetary value placed upon a felony arrest. Police are salaried. Similarly, firefighters do a great deal to protect both lives and property. Firefighting men and women do not get paid by a calculated rate according to the amount of fires they put out. Firemedics, too, are not monitored by accountants so that a pay stub may reflect a set quota of jumpstarts, intravenous sticks, or intubations. So, police are not paid by the arrest, fire personnel are not paid by the fire, and fire EMS does not get paid by the patient. Private EMS shakes out differently.

EMS is rarely supported by taxes alone. Some private firms receive partial municipal subsidies. Other private firms get complete monopolies on direct response in a given city or county for a period lasting from three to five years. EMS becomes the functional equivalent of a water company or an electric company. The city or county maintains the books, and the ambulance personnel get to concentrate on delivering care. If the bidded price of their services begins to fall short over the course of the second year, medics can be rotated into three days of direct patient care for every two days of paratransit work—work involving patient transfers from one hospital to another hospital or to a skilled nursing facility. It is difficult not to see how life and property are protected by such dedicated transports. In the 1990s, we have evolved to a point where credit card machines can be found on deluxe ambulances. In such cases, EMS is not functioning under a public safety umbrella—an umbrella that has no room for a private ambulance proxy agency.

Private EMS may not be given a municipal subsidy at all. The local fire department may in fact constitute a rival to the commercial provider. A large city in Arizona and an affluent county in

California saw this professional rivalry reduced to a bidding war in the mid-eighties. A supposed edge in efficiency on the commercial side was more than compensated for by an inviolate aura surrounding the fire service. Public safety agencies could opt to provide emergency care for free, at greatly reduced rates, or at whatever illogical level Medicare and Medicaid would permit. The most veteran fire chief might find herself annoyed at the surrealism of EMS billing.

EMS gets paid by the call. Volunteer ambulance services in eastern Pennsylvania may have subscribers, and these subscribers may pay enough money in advance to lower their bills when the need for emergency care actually does arise, but the bill is for the call, trip, run, supplies, etc. Professional services in Oklahoma would let citizens in their primary service areas subscribe to the service at an enormous discount should the occasion of a call come up, yet the discount was still predicated on the call, trip, run, etc. The same can be said about some of the operations conducted by the high profile systems where the public of a given area hire a private provider of emergency care. Non-members and paramedical transport patients are assessed according to prevailing rates (a portion of the established Medicare 75th percentile for a given area) set ultimately by federal government. Why are the police and fire services immune?

Police and fire services were considered essential by the end of the nineteenth century. They still are today. They can be distinguished from traditional emergency medical services by the fact that they do not bill by the individual units of service rendered. Unlike most EMS providers, these two more established services have ready access to excellent dispatch facilities. They enjoy superb field access to high band communications channels. On the other hand, EMS agencies must fight taxi services or bread truck fleets for trunked 800 band channels. Frequencies are blocked, and certain medical channels are loaded up by other traffic until the whole thing verges on disaster. Evidenced by a lack of respect, EMS is seldom perceived as the third essential community service.

People are not inclined to pay taxes to insure the continuation of lifesaving prehospital emergency care unless it is couched in the trappings of police, fire, firemedic, or the municipally owned hospitals. Given this sad fact of twentieth century life, it is hardly surprising that a great many EMS services have become a whole or partial subdivision of a fire suppression organization.

This has been the source of many difficulties for EMS people. Fire as EMS—or EMS becoming a part of fire—is a powerful blow to the EMS fanatic's pride. It is tantamount to admitting that EMS does not and never will command the same amount of respect as the traditional pillars of public safety, namely police and fire. EMS is just too new, or so apologists and critics both agree. EMS has yet to prove itself, or so enthusiasts and genuinely sympathetic critics could agree. It is equally possible that such voices ask too much of EMS in the first place, or that EMS promised too much too soon.

More than half of the emergency care delivered to major urban populations comes to the public by way of a fire service. Personnel are often cross-trained as both firefighters and paramedics. Since the seventies, this phenomenon has been a mixed blessing. Pay ladders and promotional opportunities were denied to fire department personnel practicing EMS. EMS was widely considered to be a punishment platoon for short-timers playing for time en route to a pension. Young people who were stuck in such platoons stayed sane by remembering that deep down below the surface they were firefighters first, last, and always. It was not uncommon to see a daytime firefighter, who functioned as a volunteer EMT or paramedic at night, feign ignorance and passionately deny these downside medical skills even when they were needed in broad daylight at the site of a major fire. "I left my EMS hat at home," says one such firefighter.

On the other hand, despite social and organizational stigmas, a combination of fire and EMS elements under one administrative heading had certain distinct advantages. Fire department discipline and traditions could be coupled with an abundance of resources in such areas as fleet maintenance, physical plant (station houses were already established in key population centers), procurement practices, and personnel administration to graft EMS onto fire service as you would a young branch to an old and deeply rooted tree. The economies of scale were and are enormous. Bulk buying from wholesalers increased the value of an EMS dollar.

EMS might well establish itself by piggybacking on the shoulders and thighs of an already accepted fire service establishment. The fire establishment should reasonably expect to gain stature and plausibly greater tax support in exchange for fostering the growth of its clinical stepchild. EMS could bask in the glory of a job well done. Fire surgeons could and did supply a modicum of medical direction—and did so as early as the sixties. Clinical protocols for fire-based EMS providers were evolved, and in some parts of the Southwest these protocols were implemented.

The EMS-fire linkage was a two way street. If EMS did lead to extra bucks in the golden seventies, then cost overruns and budget cutbacks within the fire department had a good chance of affecting EMS operations and with them the quality of emergency care. The myth that EMS operations might somehow pay for themselves to some extent by means of direct revenue was also a joker in the deck. For example, prehospital care did not always eventuate in a female on Medicare with shortness of breath who seemed to have gone into sinus ventricular tachycardia (SVT)—a female who magically survived well enough to live an additional twenty to eighty days in the hospital. The costs associated with EMS grew after 1982. The federal "miracle-oil" salespeople were gone. Fire officials had to keep EMS costs in line.

The best-known target for a cost cutting campaign was system abuse. In one particular instance in Dallas, Texas during the mid-eighties, a dispatcher call screening technique misfired badly. Physicians and other clinicians had devised a mechanism calculated to eliminate eight percent of the ambulance service requests each year. In a few short years, the screen was filtering out four times that many requests. Young fire service managers had wrested control of the screen from EMS people. In-house savings had been engineered by triaging away what might well have been valid requests for basic life support.

Suddenly, the dam broke. A man could not get an ambulance for his dying mother. The story made the network news that same night. A voice was heard asking and finally screaming while the cold and unfeeling public safety nurse dispatcher refused to offer the caller even the barest hope of an ambulance. America listened as the network depicted Fire-EMS as a callously insensitive second service seemingly engaged in the conscious betrayal of its long-stated mission. The fire service could swallow up an EMS component. This could lead to greater stores of material. There was a remote chance that it could lead to an undesirable softening of medical control. EMS saves lives, if and only if EMS listens long enough to find out where, when, and how!

In the eighties, many fire services created parallel, albeit distinct, EMS divisions for themselves in order to address both fire suppression and emergency care delivery as separate issues. It is theoretically possible for the first service to undergo a similar subdivision of labor. It could have evolved over the last two and a half decades, but it hasn't. In California, large county sheriff's departments employ EMS personnel to do a variety of jobs, but they remain police personnel. The first service might absorb EMS functions and then functionally divorce EMS from law enforcement operations. Helicopter bureaus used for medical evacuation runs at least some of the time in Maryland and New Jersey are state police operations—operations that also entail using the birds for double duty with speed enforcement runs and surveillance details. It is a great idea from the economic standpoint: one unit reflecting two cost centers. It considerably reduces the purely EMS overhead. EMS shares equipment in the provision of the first service. Police return the favor by sharing in the provision of EMS via pooled equipment, cross-trained personnel, and enhanced dispatch capabilities. The chopper comes at a much lower price, and to get this very special ambulance one would call the police—just like a forties "B" movie.

Fire service EMS is the most common form of urban EMS in the 1990s. Fire engines carry crew members who may hurry into a building with a defibrillator in hand. Do you need a hook and ladder to jumpstart a heart? Could EMS actually afford to operate without fire department resources? Indeed the fire truck on an ALS call is a familiar image from the television show "Emergency"—an image that is well-known in real terms in Los Angeles and a number of other places as well. If a bystander codes at a building fire, then there may just be somebody already on hand who can do more than your basic every day first responder.

Side by side fire and EMS is one variation—a variation wherein both elements answer to the same group of leaders. Some savings take place in terms of centralizing command functions and dispersing resources into appropriate areas. Pooled bids reduce costs for office supplies and foul-weather gear. The public is inclined to trust EMS as something akin to an extension of the well-established second service. EMS protects lives if not property, too.

EMS is comprised by a number of different organizations. Public safety is the biggest of the EMS constituents. If we turned all of it over to the fire departments, and thereby infuriated many capable professional and volunteer providers, then what would the EMS physicians say or do? The authority of the medical control physician and the resource hospital were effectively discounted a bit more than eight years ago. After all, only the most determined, selfless, and altogether uncompromising visionaries could dream of building EMS systems in which everything and everyone had a role to fulfill.

CHAPTER NINE

————— ✳ —————

The Division of Emergency Medical Services—Public Health and Critical Care Off to War

It was roughly two hundred years ago that two men set the mainspring for a tension that has animated American government ever since. Thomas Jefferson agreed with ancient Athenian theorists with regard to democracy—pure democracy is anarchy. He favored a free society—a society kept that way by being agrarian and somehow more tolerant of the rights of the individual. The discordant hippies of the sixties were born at least a century-and-a-half too late.

Alexander Hamilton was Jefferson's opposite. Hamilton subscribed to a much more orderly view of the nation's political character. Everything had its place in an ordered, more urban, and thoroughly well-organized society. The federal government would keep things from flying apart as they had briefly after the war for independence. Loosely tied former colonies nearly went a dozen different directions under a weak arrangement known as the Articles of Confederation. Hamilton wanted the federal government to play a leading role in shaping American life.

As one can readily see, the tension was enormous. Modern-day conservatives such as Ronald Reagan would no doubt please any Jeffersonians. Reagan decentralized or deregulated government functions and thereby "freed" all fifty states from the tethers of strict accountability in highway construction, health care, and savings and loan administration. Tennessee, Oregon, and Oklahoma all have derived unique experiences from America's return to very low profile federal government.

Modern-day liberals such as Senator Ted Kennedy or Senator Mark Hatfield would be equally pleasing to Hamiltonians. Entitlement programs, formula grants, and any or all efforts to impose some kind of standard from Washington, DC, or by means of the federal government's ten regional offices throughout the land, would more than fill the bill for the present-day Federalists.

It is interesting to note that America came full circle in two hundred years. Anarchistic theories handed down from Athens end in the often quoted but little understood Republican dictum that evokes the provision of essential service via "a thousand points of light." Emotional, albeit serious-minded, perspectives on the nation's ultimate destiny led ineluctably to Social Security, Medicare (but not Medicaid, as it is presently defined to favor state level options to forego legitimate participation), a national highway speed limit, a national living will act, and the abolition of a situation in which we have more than twice as many Blue Cross and Blue Shield organizations as we have states to base them in. Eighteenth century liberals and their conservative opponents would both find precisely the reverse labels applied to themselves if they were somehow magically transported across time to America circa 1992. The tension between anarchy at the one extreme and unwarranted federal interference with any or all local customs and individual freedoms at the other extreme makes America tick.

EMS systems probably shouldn't be all that anarchistic—in design if not in implementation. The organization of something so complex as EMS for the "can do" Americans of the sixties was a difficult task. The implementation of equally complicated basic life support systems for a nation enduring a "peace with honor," followed closely by nationwide television hearings that were singularly devoid of anything like honor, might have been even more difficult to accomplish. The seventies should have been anything but auspicious for a new period of social and medical reform.

EMS had hit on some enormous luck. It continued past 1982 into the aftermath of systemization. A catalyst was needed. Someone or something had to inspire the reaction that would set all the right wheels in motion. This motion would in turn bring about the desired reaction in a borderline defeatist nation. The need was real.

Nobody had quite forgotten "can do" yet. A president from Georgia together with the humiliation of American hostages in Iran were required before the ache of impotence crept into certain portions of the American national consciousness. A sense of incompleteness vied for control with leftover remembrances of a vigorous, prodigious, and extremely pragmatic nation. Some things were still possible. Basic Life Support EMS Systems were destined to be one of them. A catalytic agent had surfaced at what proved to be the opportune time.

Enter the quarterback of many a losing football team—Dr. David R. Boyd. He has learned from his experiences on the gridiron, and many years later he is enriched by different experiences in the foremost trauma center in American history. David Boyd studied and grew at Dr. R. Adams Cowley's state-supported Maryland shock trauma center. The large specialty center was popularly known for a distinguishing landmark—a large red garbage dumpster that scores of medevac patients would pass en route from the top of the parking garage (a.k.a. heliport) to the team waiting behind the swinging doors of the trauma intensive care unit. The center was also known for its innovations—some of them brought to light by way of Austria. Dog labs and some valid scientific insight into the nature of cell death and its relationship to perfusion put the trauma-oriented EMS system on the map. In the late eighties and early nineties, Tom Clancy's novel *Patriot Games* celebrated the justifiable mystique surrounding this shrine to "can do" for hundreds of thousands of non-EMS readers. Not far from a red dumpster, the catalyst was honing his temperament.

Boyd went on to seek further enlightenment through some additional time at Cook County Hospital in a most inhospitable part of Chicago. "Care delayed" equated with "care denied" struck a familiar chord within him as he labored in the urban equivalent of a military MASH unit. Trained initially as a physician at McGill University in Montreal, and now seasoned by urban tours, he arose from the squalor as the very incarnation of the "cutting doc."

The surgeon confronted the American medical establishment with a pithy doctrine drawn from a rather certain vision of needless deaths. Many people died because they had been taken to the wrong place. This was true in Maryland and Illinois, and must have been true elsewhere in the United States! The concept of unnecessary death was elevated a few notches to include a bad choice of facilities, a bad choice of treatment modalities on the scene, and worse still, very bad schemata for configuring almost everything that ought to be included in the local EMS systems. David R. Boyd threw gauntlets down much more surely than he had ever flung passes to his wide receivers. The first round against unnecessary death took place in Illinois.

The leaders of Illinois were dealing to an undeniably brilliant zealot. Dr. Boyd donned his blue buttondown shirt—a shirt that was to become his trademark. He proceeded to hurl a well-aimed challenge at those who made EMS systems all but impossible. The list of targets included complacent physicians, smug hospital administrators, shortsighted bureaucrats both inside and outside of the federal government, nominal emergency room physicians, dispirited nurses, and wholly untrained prehospital personnel. It seemed that EMS had its very own Napoleon Bonaparte. In reality, EMS had someone analogous to a figure from a slightly early period in French history—Citizen Robespierre. David R. Boyd, MDCM was hell-bent on preaching, and at the same time practicing, revolution.

And where better from which to attack the establishment than from a perch securely inside that very same establishment? The American Left of the sixties and the early seventies had always dreamed of purifying or perverting the centers of power by co-opting them from the inside. The hippies reasoned that confrontation could thereby be avoided. A small but fanatical cadre might have to submerge under the veneer of grey suits, but they would have to win out in the final reckoning. Dr. Boyd was not a typical protester of the Vietnam era; he had a much different war in mind.

Somewhere along the line, during the course of his training in Montreal, Dr. Boyd began to formulate a mental sketch of the type of strategy one would have to employ to make a meaningful impact on unnecessary death. Like many technocratic physicians trained to fight disease scientifically, as opposed to treating the patients like individuals, the Illinois EMS director focused his informed intellect on a disease closely associated with at least 115,000 deaths nationally each year, a third of which might have been avoided. His enemy drew strength from mismanaged emergency care resources, inappropriate emergency care resources, or the concrete lack of such resources. Failing to deliver the right kind of care could and did result in the preventable deaths of potentially salvageable patients.

He demonstrated that concept by redirecting patient flow in and around Mt. Vernon, Illinois. The death rates for males under the age of fifty-five declined with appropriate patient placement and subsequent care. Reconfiguring the entire health care delivery system to prevent unnnecessary death made perfect sense. If it could work in Mt. Vernon, Illinois, it must work nationally—and not just for traumatic injuries born of motor vehicle accidents! Dr. Boyd had to reorder the known universe of critical care, while at the same time blunting the unbelievable influence of public safety on EMS.

He would run the risk of being eaten alive in a many-tiered hornet's nest. When the call came inviting Illinois's revolutionary thinker to Washington, and with it the opportunity to do the whole thing all over again on a national scale, how could he refuse? Cast by Fate and his own nature in the role of renegade director of a rogue agency, and finding quite quickly that the role suited him, Dr. Boyd molded the Division of Emergency Medical Services into a small strike force and set out on an eight-year odyssey—seeking a universal home for critically emergent patients. Cutting across the grain of American life meant heartaches, hints of sabotage from within, the inevitable medical retirements, those externally imposed limits on internal stability (accomplished by refusal to grant permanent job titles and the frequent rotation of USPHS and USCG personnel in and out of perpetual vacancies), the growth of an all-consuming passion for Dr. Boyd's war, and the utter loss of both heart and soul by the devotees of that same war. If Robespierre was caught up in the French Revolution, and unwittingly became blind to its excesses, then Dr. Boyd and his closest followers might well have fallen prey to something similar in the long run.

It had all begun innocently enough. In September of 1966, Public Law 89-564, a highway safety act, was passed. The law authorized planning for ambulances and the equipment to go in them (see Chapter 10). The focus was on prehospital care, but it did touch on such key areas as personnel and communications. Section 402 matched state monies set aside for highway safety purposes. Section 403 funded research and other demonstration projects. More than half a billion dollars was generated at the state level over the course of a dozen or so years.

Dr. Daniel Moynihan, then of Massachusetts Institute of Technology, was not about to cede to DOT the hegemony over almost anything that might some day amount to medically accountable systems of emergency care. He convinced President Nixon of the wisdom of expanded federal involvement in EMS. Training conferences were held in 1969 and 1971. In a subsequent state of the union address, Nixon went so far as to lament a seeming epidemic of accidental deaths.

Since President Nixon had committed himself to better health care systems while addressing the 92nd Congress, EMS people took him at his word and edged the government toward a greater commitment to EMS systems development. A nationwide regional medical program initiative had appropriated almost eleven million dollars to EMS between 1970 and 1972. The National Academy of Sciences had long pressured for a national level EMS Council to be housed directly within the executive branch. Skeptics were to be mollified by the approval of sixteen million dollars for more definitive EMS demonstration projects. Mental health administrators with the public health bureaucracy oversaw the work done in Arkansas, California, northeastern Florida, Appalachian Ohio, and Illinois.

The demonstrations were ostentatious at times, but they contributed to a growing EMS consciousness in state and local government circles. This increased awareness was both facilitated and broadened by more narrowly focused EMS development projects in thirty-two states—projects sanctioned by the Robert Wood Johnson Foundation with much energy for a mere handful of years. The stage was just about set in August 1973. Everything was ready— everything except for the lead player/director. President Nixon had a number of distractions keeping him away from the play. Unwelcome publicity had started to come Nixon's way beginning in March. The following August would see such publicity come to a boil, and the subsequent heat would drive Richard M. Nixon from the White House. President Nixon might use the Watergate crisis as an explanation for temporizing on a wide number of policy issues. EMS was not one of them. In August of 1973, President Nixon vetoed a bill that would establish a federally inspired formula for EMS systems development. Not even the artful intercession of Gerald Ford could help Senate Bill 504.

The beleaguered President stated that he didn't need another federal program employing dollars to disrupt state and local EMS system development activities—whatever and wherever they might be. Somewhere the ghost of Jefferson was smiling! Representative

Gerry Ford rescued the EMS legislation from disaster after Congress had failed to overturn President Nixon's veto. In the early fall of 1973, the man slated to take Nixon's place in less than a year's time edited the bill to exclude its provision for a few new hospitals. And the rest is history.

Public Law 93-154 went into effect on November 16, 1973. It created a Title 12 Administration which was initially funded at $185 million for three years. One of the more idealistic provisions was one that forbade the denial of emergency care on the basis of inability to pay. The legislation was renewed twice more in the seventies—PL 94-573 in 1976 and PL 96-142 in 1979. It was negated, rejected, or shall we say all but obliterated by a Preventive Health Services Block Grant scheme known to wounded souls everywhere as PL 97-35 (1981).

At one of the most unlikely and inauspicious moments in American history, some of the diehard dreamers among the many people reflecting on the fall of Saigon or the genocide in neighboring Cambodia, had managed to get the adrenalin surging in the sinews of countless war-scarred tissues in order to mount still another campaign to save mankind. Causes were in disrepute, and this one had a rough row to hoe.

The annointed leader for a crusade against unnecessary death and a growing failure to do anything at all at the national level was Dr. Boyd. He came to the DC area by way of Washington state, Quebec, Maryland, and Illinois to survey the nation from what he soon made the pinnacle of EMS system development in all the land, and perhaps even the world. Dr. Boyd knew the score was about twenty-one to zero in the second quarter, and so it was time to start hurling a flurry of long and short passes down the field. The Division of Emergency Medical Services had been created by Title 12 legislation. Dr. Boyd found that a limited retinue came with the helm of DEMS. The unit was staffed by a small cadre of provisionally appointed civil servants, complimented by an even smaller number of untouchable permanent USPHS staff. Clearly, it would be hard to make the existing health care delivery structures tremble through the efforts of a comparative handful of core staff personnel.

DEMS circumvented this obstacle by skillfully applying the golden rule. Lauding the gleaming coffers over the heads of ten federal regions chock-full of grantees yielded the following: physician technical advisors for each of eight critical care categories; regional technical assistance people serving in such areas as telecommunications; and special consultants performing duties in such fields as independent evaluation or the more arcane circular, horizontal, and vertical categorization. Dr. Boyd drew on the expertise of seasoned veterans from Illinois. He combined them with a growing pool of brilliant newcomers from all over the nation. He called upon his revolutionary intelligentsia to inspire, educate, and inculcate the very real sense of something larger at stake in every conference, technical assistance meeting, quarterly report by a grantee to the regional DEMS authorities, and in each and every piece of the much-admired gold. Teresa Romano and Winny Pizzano translated the nursing lessons of a categorized Trauma-EMS system in Illinois into a call for action at the grantee level. Ranking hospitals and patients, and finding an appropriate match was deceptively simple.

When the show ended, the grant staff had to go home, play the same tune in front of the home folks, and do a certain amount of contortions to bend existing establishments until they approximated the pristine reality of DEMS's program guidelines. Dr. Costas Lambrew was the leading showperson and bona fide superstar in the medical control area. He left Maine on trips to Dr. Boyd's shows in order to share in the genius of what he had accomplished much earlier in Nassau County, New York. Professor Geoffrey Gibson of Johns Hopkins University, together with Dr. C. Gene Cayten, a physician researcher from the Wharton School at the University of Pennsylvania, provided guidance on the problems associated with evaluating EMS systems and the performance of EMS personnel.

In strictly clinical areas, the spokespeople and their licit federal DEMS sanctioned views often met with entrenched or even strident resistance. Dr. Bernard Linn, working from a base in Florida, argued that many moderate burn cases could be treated in community hospitals and would emerge just fine without having the benefit of a Level One dedicated specialty center. In poison cases, many critics believed that patients were more in need of management by an information network than an elaborate set of hospital levels. Sophisticated and urban medical trade areas questioned the need for cardiac resource hospitals. Why control cardiac care in the prehospital phase when there are eight medical schools with 500-bed hospitals ready to assume least indirect medical responsibility for each patient within a ten minute radius of their emergency rooms? Trauma as argued for Orange County versus San Francisco was put forth by Dr. Donald Trunkey and Dr. John West. Their initial study was repeated twice because critics could not accept the simplicity of an argument favoring trauma centers over care rendered, according to normal or chance patterns of patient flow in an affluent medical trade area. Patient placement criteria just couldn't be that important.

Learned rejection was understandable up to a point, and literate resistance made a certain amount of sense, but conscious refusals to follow the implications of plausible and possibly beneficial plans of action were unfortunate. In certain regions of the country, such adamant parochialism was the rule rather than the exception. If Mississippi or New Hampshire could be made to fit the mold, then New York City or Boston would not be made to fit anything. Political pull put the bite on Dr. Boyd's bosses in the health care bureaucracy. Evaluation of a region's progress by an independent observer gave way to assessments by home-grown observers. The Federal District Office managers brought a number of unique twists to the implementation of Dr. Boyd's overall theme. Communications in New England had little in common with the techniques being employed in Alabama.

It appeared to many confused or embittered local folks that DEMS was just another game—tap dance until they throw you some pieces of gold. One could designate a specialty center as DEMS-funded, and then collect as little data as possible in compliance with mandates suggesting that certain types of patients belonged in that center, while claiming in a quarterly report filed with the federal region's DEMS office that EMS systemization was going forward in and around that facility. One could collect grant monies to improve communications capabilities, fuss with representatives from three different vendors, and then proceed to implement these much needed improvements as slowly as humanly possible. In short, EMS providers could gather up Dr. Boyd's gold without bothering to remember what it was supposed to buy.

Wondrous visions, frightened bureaucrats, intransigent but conniving locals, and maybe a few medical people with an honest difference of opinion made for interesting times. Ivy League-trained epidemiologists did postgraduate work under the tutelage of seasoned grantee staff—staff that was pretty much in the habit of building and inventing better mousetraps. Bold physicians did what they could to insure that the gold would pass to the local regions in manner that would redound to the credit of the Title 12 Administration (a.k.a. DEMS). Surgeons became EMTs and injected a note of wildness into system building. The catalysts emerged quickly. The true believers and their local audiences had to bite down hard on the bit in order to comprehend a seemingly endless array of changes.

Patient-tracking was mandated long before anyone knew what data-gathering and management information systems actually entailed. Critical care abstracts were applied as measurement tools to such scientific areas as mutual aid agreements, consumer participation, and standardized recordkeeping. People counted the number of EMTs trained each year without bothering to determine how many graduated successfully from that training. Applied research and planning workbooks were tried as a sure shot crash course in EMS system development. It was a mad dash for the stars until the time of the second renewal of the EMSS Act in 1979.

Extravagances, both imagined and real, were targeted for elimination at that time. Research became evaluation research. Professionals were interested in trauma tracer analyses of motor vehicle accident head injuries. People attempted outcome measurement of the care rendered to EMS impactable cardiac cases in the prehospital and hospital phases of emergency care. As times grew harsher, and the "can do" withered while rumors circulated about the subcultural ties of the White House Press Secretary, EMS people persisted in the belief that they could and should reform acute care, critical care, and prehospital care in America. Burns and spinal cord injuries were buried under the heading of traumas. Since the data surrounding advanced life support care was equivocal in its implications, and this was especially true as it applied to cardiacs, the major emphasis of systemization efforts after 1979 became trauma-EMS systems. EMS systems were to be built around trauma centers.

Trauma centers were automatically given the mantle of medical control resource hospitals. After October of 1980, grant seekers in all of the 304 eligible regions had to at least go through the motions of designating Level One Trauma Centers in order to qualify for even one dime of Dr. Boyd's money. Many of them did it.

Many more of them begged off on the final rounds of golden rule roulette.

From 1974 through 1981, DEMS brought 171 of the 304 EMS regions up to snuff—"snuff" being the capacity to configure organized resources to deliver basic life support care. About a third of the regions aspired to configurations centered around advanced life support care. DEMS studied its own effectiveness with computer models primed by data abstracts from all funded regions.

The data came from Illinois, Connecticut, Oakland, California, Iowa, Oregon, Hanover, New Hampshire, Concord, New Hampshire, Newark, New Jersey, Liverpool, New York, and in a much smaller way from places like Biloxi, Mississippi. Regions with five years of funding behind them toughed it out with regions with little or no background in organizing EMS. This resulted in resentment on both sides. The upstarts snatched financial nourishment from the delicate, albeit talented, veterans. Political pressure from influential Senators and Congresspersons sometimes gave DEMS grant awards the trappings of a sweetheart contract. In effect, the golden rule was a collusion with the influential.

In the final analysis, it was something of a tradeoff. As DEMS tried to co-opt the Health Resource Administration and the Health Service Administration, and thereby obtain a foothold from which to remodel acute care, the EMS regions used elected officials to blunt the intensity of Dr. Boyd's revolutionary zeal. Research and science were just additional reporting requirements—requirements that almost nobody linked to practices in the hospital or out in the field. The data indicated that more than half of the regions had reduced their regional death rates from emergent conditions by following Dr. Boyd's party line—a line encapsulated by the categorization of hospitals, triage protocols, and the appropriate placement of patients. DEMS had achieved a national network for basic life support by 1981. Just as the case had been in Mount Vernon, Illinois, back when Dr. Boyd was making noises from a smaller perch, EMSS reduced the regional death rate for some conditions after only three years of effort. But the fourth and fifth years presented DEMS with a monumental point of diminishing returns! Progressing to advanced life support capability was no mean feat in 1980. EMS kept very sick patients alive long enough for them to die in the hospital instead of in the field. Scientific research found little difference between advanced life support and basic life support. One was cheaper; both seemed to deliver the same amount of live bodies for discharge from the hospital. Paramedic care in 1980 did not feature more than fifty drugs on board the ambulance, MICU, or fly car. Basic life support was a safer promise to make, if EMS promised no more than it could deliver.

Science, revolution, and pure zeal had an effective end limit after all. In 1981, DEMS could go no farther than basic life support systems. Paramedics were a largely unseen, untested, and unproven resource throughout much of the country. By that time DEMS didn't have to worry about it, for EMSS-Title 12 had been phased out. The wholesale abandonment of this successful experiment was carefully masked by sliding EMS under the auspices of Preventive Health Block Grants. The nominal assumption was that a public health presence in the EMS field would survive a battle against rape awareness and rat control.

In 1982, Dr. Boyd was trying to relocate some of his vast library holdings to a university near his Maryland home. DEMS was gone, and the revolutionary banner was furled once again. DEMS had accomplished much in a rather short amount of time, but most of America no longer cared. One element that did care was a rival, and at times antagonistic, agency a few miles down the road from Dr. Boyd's one-time base—an agency situated squarely in DC proper.

CHAPTER TEN

———— ✳ ————

The National Highway Traffic Safety Administration— Longevity and the Art of Compromise

A network of interstate highways was a cherished goal of a great society. Moreover, it can be said that transportation capabilities separate civilized (a.k.a. citified) societies from the developing tribal organizations of the third world. Organized commerce and the timely transportation of manufactured goods brought Europe out of a veritable stone age as early as the twelfth century. The awakening of Europe continued until the middle of the fourteenth century. Around 1349, the whole thing came to an abrupt end when the bubonic plague brought about acute labor shortages, due to the death of many of the farm personnel. People in the cities had little to eat and nobody to sell their crafts to in the now very open markets. The French had only recently freed all the serfs, and the population of the cities had become swollen. In Holland, there were bread lines much like their American counterparts six hundred years later.

The late medieval market managers were forced to return to manorial farms in order to play a leading role in feeding the fortunate generation of plague survivors. The moral might be that one cannot emancipate one's serfs unless one receives divine or actuarial assurances that there won't be some pestilence killing as much as seventy percent of the work force. A more noteworthy corollary, at least for our purposes, is that transportation makes a better life possible.

Railroads changed the course of nineteenth century American life. They put an end to the cattle baron and gunslinger culture so popular in American literature and American, German, and Italian movies—movies that are equally or even more popular in Europe where America is seen as a cowboy society all grown up. The next blow to the stillness of the wide open spaces came by way of a low-cost automobile. Henry Ford's mass-produced and relatively afford-able automobile made life in the saddle a great deal less necessary at the beginning of the twentieth century. White, male Americans were suddenly free to travel and explore the world around them. Women faced cultural barriers to such free-spirited behavior. Afri-can Americans had their world circumscribed by different barri-ers—barriers that had been reinforced by a U.S. Supreme Court decision during the last decade of the nineteenth century that paved the way for the view that African Americans should grow up going to school in a country consisting of separate but equal facili-ties for the mainstream. African Americans were to choose their roads carefully. A journey by car could end up in a fatal "accident."

The vehicles themselves were reasonably sturdy. The roads were not usually macadamized. This was destined to change for the better. An increasingly urbanized and industrialized America came to require more cars and better roads on which to drive them. Road construction gangs consisting of hordes of unemployed people living in work camps were used to advance the cause of a national network of excellent roads for a time during the horribly depressed period of Franklin Roosevelt's first two terms as president. The war against Hitler clearly demonstrated that good highways facilitated the rapid movement and subsequent timely positioning of troops. The lesson was not lost on American leaders involved in a "Cold War" with the Soviet Union.

In theory, American troops had to be able to move on the ground from Erie, Pennsylvania to New York City in a short period of time. A wide four- to six-lane interstate highway would facilitate the movement of defending troops along a real or imagined inter-nal axis. This type of highway could have its uses for anyone or anything still functioning after both antagonists in a nuclear war had actually gone on with launching both first and second nuclear strikes.

In 1964, you could find yourself stuck behind an ICBM being escorted by military police and air force personnel, as it meandered with some difficulty along the roads in the White or Green Mountains toward one of the rare north-south highways in New Hampshire and Vermont. In 1977, Americans had tanks so heavy that they would crack the paved highways leading from Fort Knox to Louisville or Bardstown, Kentucky. As time wore on, and technology brought us better missiles and lasers, the practical value of the interstate highway system for anything less than the period after a nuclear apocalypse was called into question. After all, helicopters and transport planes could do a great deal for the brigadier looking for an internal axis for defense—a defense, which was being established in an era when the attacking armies might hope to advance at least fifty miles in a single day. Nevertheless, in the 1980s, the popular association of transportation with war, destruction, and survivalist ethics found expression in feature films.

Australian actor Mel Gibson played a one-eyed, slightly mad former police officer saving what is left of Western civilization after a nuclear war. This movie (*The Road Warriors*) version of civilization was dominated by vehicle owners racing down highways in quest of reservoirs or other storage facilities for refined fossil fuels. In a sequel (*Beyond Thunderdome*), the hero delivers children, who are leftover from a wartime plane crash to the new home of civilization—a totally depopulated but physically intact Sydney, Australia. The motif was also used in the movie, *Hell Comes to Frogtown*, where a popular kilt-wearing wrestler (Roddy Piper) was cast as a virile male in a mostly sterile universe. The wrestler uses transportation to traverse a wasteland and deliver the human race from reptile mutants bent on destroying it.

Although the nuclear devastation angle is more than a little negative, and is sometimes trivialized by the television shows which feature innocent but illegal commandos fighting for the underdog and against evil and/or the government, it ought to be abundantly clear that transportation, and particularly automobiles, form the basis for romantic fantasies and boundless dreams. Rock songs in the pre-war sixties argued for the merits of particular cars. They also spoke of the drivers—a category that included ice cream truck operators and hot-footed grandmothers. Yuppies in the eighties found that their vehicles were status symbols. Materialistic, if not egocentristic, young adults rediscovered much of the world that their hippie parents had "tripped out" to avoid. The car came back into the limelight. A novel by Stephen King that became a movie gave a car all the attributes of a horror film villian. The dashboard became, in a couple of ways, a ball game in a popular countercultural rocker's first mainstream success. And the rockabillies were born in a moving interstate bus! Cry as economists might about the need to get away from a dependence on foreign oil, and cry they did in 1973 during a putative oil embargo of that year, the American romance with the open road was too much of an integral facet of the American character to be changed any time soon.

The fact that Americans drove too fast or drank too much liquor and beer in pursuit of this romance of the highway were traits that some of Dr. Boyd's most interesting neighbors had been put in business to change. The National Academy of Sciences openly rejoiced in the mid-sixties when the Congress put together an action group for duty on the accidental death as a neglected disease front. The Academy's report of a three-year research commission frequently expressed the hope that transportation managers and traffic safety engineers would rescue America from so many needless deaths. The action group had little if anything in common with Boyd's DEMS. It came into existence nearly a decade before DEMS. It posed no threat to the acute care sector or, for that matter, physician groups. Highway construction monies were a bit different from entitlement programs or formula grants. A great deal of the emergency care related funds came to a state by way of its governor's highway safety representative. Engineers got politicos to approve injury reduction measures.

It would hardly play well on either the Hamiltonian or Jeffersonian sides of the hall. Could big government do it all? Big government could fail to intervene. But there was a middle ground between the two sides. A nineteenth century pre-Civil War master of compromise known as Henry Clay would have enjoyed seeing the Department of Transportation's National Highway Traffic Safety Administration's EMS Bureau in action. NHTSA's EMS group gave money to the states. The states matched these funds under the headings of 402 and 403 grants (see Chapter 9). The federal and state officials had almost an equal stake in launching these ventures, since dollars had to be put up in order to get dollars in return. Both ends of the equation had to be balanced or nothing whatsoever would happen.

In truth, about a half a billion dollars worth of something happened. EMT standards were perfected, paramedic standards were invented, and vehicles were purchased for the EMTs and the paramedics to use when responding to calls.

Nobody can deny that DOT was there first. The DOT EMS chieftan, Leo Schwartz, had a shop in place long before a noisy, seemingly inconsiderate, and downright mercurial cousin sprang to life under Dr. David R. Boyd. In the eyes of the revolutionaries, EMS might be more than just ambulances and standardized training. Schwartz and company funded EMS systems research. They located a group of what later proved to be very talented health care researchers in the Industrial Engineering Department of the University of Pittsburgh. EMS was thought of as a systems or technical problem, not a medical one. Safeguarding the romance of the road required algorithms. It might just be that the transportation side of EMS was the logical target for adept engineers. Other targets were injury prevention campaigns, the techniques used to train emergency care personnel, and the impact of better techniques on the long-term field performance of different classes of emergency care personnel.

Needless to say, this eminently pragmatic approach was quite different from that of the more flamboyant visionaries at the Division of Emergency Medical Services. A bureaucratic turf fight broke out before the first renewal of the EMS Systems Act. It continued right up until the last two weeks that Dr. David R. Boyd spent in the service of what was then called the Department of Health, Education and Welfare. Many blamed it all on Dr. Boyd's wild, yet commanding, personality. The line goes that EMS's answer to Citizen Robespierre elicited personal and professional antagonism from the stern, stoical, and monistic people trying to engineer injury prevention. There are countless other ways to explain it all away. The most customary method has been to sweep it all under some proverbial rug—a rug that official historians must keep on hand for such dire emergencies. It is nothing less than absurd for us to go on ignoring one of the most pivotal periods in American EMS history.

More than eight hundred million dollars hung in the balance as DEMS and the older NHTSA EMS unit went to war. DEMS was considered by its opponent to be an interloper. NHTSA was considered wholly deficient in "clinical background." Training was DOT's forte. Critical care patient placements were an EMS system's issue. DOT's moderate masters of compromise, deeply situated in the win/win-brokered relationship with many of the fifty governors' highway safety representatives, fought for stability. They hoped to achieve better EMS by virtue of a slow evolutionary process.

DEMS's wild seers, lacking in federal civil service tenures, and numbering not much more than thirty at any given time, had to work instead through a network of grantee staffers of uneven quality. They fought for a reordering of acute care and, by extension, prehospital care. They had to create or improve EMS by means of a fast and nearly explosive imposition of a new order from the high ranks in accordance with the golden rule. Finesse and guile had to take a back seat to flashiness, bravado, naked courage, and the constant game between the established medical power centers. The object of the game was to cajole, bribe, entice, and overwhelm until unnecessary death was on the run and a systematic ordering of both hospitals and patients was tenuously in place.

Engineers supporting evolution and science were pitted against medical revolutionaries trying to overcome very steep odds in order to overturn the existing makeshift arrangements in the field and inside the emergency rooms. It was a contest between rival temperaments and antithetical perspectives. In the end, NHTSA outlasted DEMS.

It survived to continue its brokering of a place for the federal government in local EMS systems from 1982 through 1990. The war ruined the "can do" climate for many EMS people. The lack of a clear consensus in the field began to haunt one and all as early as 1979. Brokering replaced the eager anticipaion of dramatic results. Burn care was elevated to an unbelievably prestigious level as the EMS Systems Act was renewed yet again. The revolutionary ardor was being dampened by the ever-present tradition of accommodation. The war left scars, and had lasting effects. Some of these effects were:

1) a lasting confusion over what the federal government's role in emergency medical service systems was really going to be;

2) a divorce between the hospital side of EMS and the prehospital side of EMS;

3) an exaggerated sense that you had to "prove" that your brand of emergency care delivery was the best;

4) a palpable uneasiness between serious trailblazing surgeons and what appeared to be brasher colleagues within the ranks of the emergency care physicians;

5) a lingering antipathy toward the idea that exclusively paramedic systems were too expensive and largely unproven;

6) a winnowing process by virtue of which the idea of steady progress toward a fixed goal fell by the wayside and scattered;

7) a distrust of regional EMS councils or most anything regional in nature;

8) the perception that Dr. Boyd's DEMS brought with it a plague of insensitive locusts determined to make marionettes of one and all, dancing on a five to seven year string;

9) the notion that NHTSA provided a steady and dependable set of functionaries with the ability to pork barrel monies slated for preventing injuries.

In its bare essentials, both sides in the war did their best to discredit the other. The public health element became an implied antagonist for the public safety element. The specialty physician came to disparage the non-physician or even the less specialized physician. How could civilians interfere with the practice of medicine? Dr. Boyd might interfere, or a notable of the American College of Emergency Practice physicians from North Carolina could propose an alternative scheme for categorizing hospitals. But where did NHTSA come off using industrial engineers? How could anyone on the outside freely accept the garbled messages from the EMS world circa 1977–1982?

The war had to end. Dr. Boyd's assault on the established order would pass. DOT would survive by blending itself into the matrix of grant recipients, and NHTSA blended itself to the point that it was hard to pick it out against the background of fifty feudal kingdoms.

Dr. Boyd's movement was in its death throes from 1982 to 1984. A central authority for EMS matters in Washington died with it. Nobody ever tried to make the whole nation practice systematic emergency care again. Why should they? The tide ran toward abolishing government as much as possible. The leaders of federal government bureaus had to know that it was most unwise to buck that tide. This was certainly the case with NHTSA. Carefully evolving concepts were poised to resist centrifugal forces, parochialism, fragmentation among participating elements of Dr. Boyd's old systems, and worse yet, comparative obscurity.

NHTSA was less a dynamic center of federal EMS policy than a congenial source of money and an understanding ear. They sought to sustain vestiges of a national EMS umbrella in the face of a domestic health policy drought. After all, NHTSA understood training needs. Five years later, it was determined that several thousand rescue squad personnel could be grandfathered into the EMT ranks of a given state because local officials had expressed the hope that they would take a legitimate refresher course several years later. Longevity has its price! Where did Dr. Boyd's fanatic idealism get him? As President Reagan phased out a number of the national government's functions, and as Dr. Boyd's former evaluation coordinator took the helm for the retiring Leo Schwartz, NHTSA found new ways to stay in the EMS game.

One way was to work closely with the Civilian Disease Control Center personnel to combat trauma as a disease in its epidemic stages. Grants for trauma-related research were awarded on a competitive basis to the best researchers in the land. Research focusing on the quantification of traumatic injuries was considered to be a cornerstone for the formulation of any future policy concerning trauma at the national level. The scholars applied severity scales to patient data, and used the results to effectively predict the mortality and long term mobility associated with traumatic injuries (see Chapter 13). The best known of these inventive researchers were Dr. Howard Champion, Ellen Mackenzie, Susan Baker, William Sacco, and Dr. C. Gene Cayten. They have worked throughout the last decade to perfect their techniques. All have been encouraged by NHTSA's "stick-to-it" attitude and have gone on to accurately depict the anatomical and physiological dimensions of traumatic injuries.

A second avenue for keeping up a bold front at a time of declining interest was an attempt at standardization by way of the back door. NHTSA received DOT backing to launch an initiative in the middle of the 1980s. The American Society for Testing and Materials Committee F-30 considered EMS to be an industry that could be regulated by standards agreed upon by participating members of the affected industry itself. The group process or delphi panel consensus method of evolving standards had obvious appeal for NHTSA. The ideas was that everybody left in the EMS industry who cared about a given topic would be locked in the same room and would have to argue the merits of the extremist or centrist position until a standard emerged! If that failed a series of ballots would be mailed to them until a standard evolved. The process was very democratic; no special interest is forgotten, and no single special interest is dominant. Even Jefferson might have been proud.

The idea found expression in large working committees. By 1990, these committees were totally devoid of physicians empowered to represent the established physician groups of the United States. Physician groups *en masse* turned a deaf ear to ASTM F-30 because "lay people could not regulate the practice of medicine." Ironically, both physician groups and individual physicians who had opposed Dr. Boyd were now in the position of refuting the concept that lay people could dictate medical practices. While it is true that NHTSA-inspired F-30 had a wide assortment of views on management, communications, training, and evaluation, and that the physicians participated long enough to arrive at a standard for the critical care of burns, the fact of the matter is that almost all of the doctors got up and went.

Voluntary standards are something like a housing development built solely of playing cards. They are hard to locate and very difficult to imagine. There have been some minor miracles. It would also seem that the initial impetus has not been translated into anything like a sustained momentum.

NHTSA survived. Seat belt laws were passed. Speed limits were lowered to fifty-five miles per hour, only to be raised again when the price at the pump declined. EMS fragmented further into a wide number of variations on a select number of themes. Nowhere were these variations more apparent than in the nation's major cities.

CHAPTER ELEVEN

───────── ✳ ─────────

Pittsburgh, Seattle, and New York

Urban EMS is something special. The demand for care can exceed the known supply of caregivers. In terms of delivering emergency care, this dilemma has no easy solution. Failure to find a way out of it leads inexorably to Dr. Boyd's old nemisis, unnecessary death. Bad planning that results in insufficient resources borders on murder, or so the traditional DEMS rhetoric claimed!

Around 1979, Trauma-EMS systems doctrine, as put forth by Dr. Boyd's shop, suggested in the strongest possible terms that a failure to bypass a lower level of care with a very sick trauma patient was tantamount to a systems failure. Moral truisms were easily arrived at before diagnosis-related groups and economic diversions made for a tremendous insult to the urban acute care sector in the 1980s. It was at this point that the demand for EMS outstripped the available supply. In fact, the need for all types of health care has grown so exponentially between 1982 and today that it has reached the point of being unmeasurable. More services are required than the health planners could ever hope to estimate with linear charts or non-linear regression models. The progression toward an almost unlimited health care need is virtually geometrical. The ramifications of being unable to service that need are stark, horrifying, and likely to endow physicians and paramedics alike with a sense of futility. Many of the caregivers will find deeper refuge in the harsh crust that accompanies futility—a type of emotional body armor often prescribed for a predilection toward overall impotence. The more you are exposed to it, the more you tend toward burnout, heartbreak, or the sense that much of your professional life is spent pitching shovel after shovel of sand at a huge and murky flood tide.

Not surprisingly, the greatest incidence of shooting yourself in the foot clinically occurs in cities. Urban EMS people seldom have long to wait to perform some serious business. Urban areas have been historically the hubs of all kinds of trade, so why not health, or more specifically, EMS?

In the last part of the Middle Ages, European cities developed along important transportation routes or at crossroads. Markets and fairs conducted episodically, and later continuously, outside the city's wall gave rise to newer sections of the city. Transportation and commerce made it possible for the city dwellers to become artisans, craftspersons, or merchants. The farmers or their overlords sold the foodstuffs needed to sustain the city's population. In Portugal and Holland, fishing provided as much or more food than the farmers. Disease wiped out more people in the cities because of the sheer proximity of people to one another. Sanitation had been a major public health concern of Moors living in southern Spain prior to the fourteenth century. Cities can mean garbage. Garbage can mean rats and the disease-carrying parasites that rats play host to on their travels.

Cities would seem like a natural locale for health care delivery modalities. In the medieval Granada or present-day Los Angeles, the logic is inescapable. Public health ought to be where the action is likely to be found. Many people live in cities, and when they get sick or injured they seek medical attention there. American cities were populated by artisans, craftspeople, working people from mills and factories, generations of recently arrived immigrants beginning around the 1840s, former farmers displaced by glutted markets or improper banking practices, or by improper land management practices, particularly in the South. Until the first world war, sick city dwellers sought care directly from physicians. The physicians had a wide range of training backgrounds. America had a great variety of medical schools—schools with widely divergent courses of study. It was pot luck.

Physician education took definitive form about the same time that the physician began to move much of her or his medical practice into a hospital setting. The result was a familiar pattern in which the urban dwellers often found their way into hospitals in order to obtain hospital-based physician care. Some places developed ambulance care capabilities earlier than others. New York had lady fire surgeons roaming northern Manhattan and the lower Bronx in horse-drawn wooden wagons long before physicians with six years of college, using hospitals for complicated cases, became an accepted source of quality medical care. The city was an intense, concentrated site of many institutions of higher learning.

Philadelphia had a medical school before Thomas Jefferson ever took office. Many medical schools began as small businesses—businesses colored by the intellectual fetishes of their nineteenth century founders. You could learn to cure a patient by using copious amounts of water. Medicine did not acquire a lasting scientific halo until the 1920s. In a free society, a great many things are possible. It is important to consider that in 1991, some urban Americans still go doctor shopping. A few of their neighbors might well prefer chiropractors to orthopedists.

By 1964, the dust cloud produced by America's hospital, physician, and education groups when they forcefully imposed a species of order on American medical practices had pretty well dissipated. Emergency rooms had already begun to serve as surrogates for the family physician in the city and the suburbs. Hospital-based paramedics and fire paramedics were well on their way off the driving board and into reality. Cities were pivotal proving grounds for EMS from 1964 to the present. The burden of proof could be lifted right here as nowhere else. The need was great, the demand was identifiable, and the stakes were high.

PITTSBURGH

A filthy steel manufacturing center spent much of the twentieth century choked by clouds of soot. Originally the site of a fort that protected the confluence of three rivers, and a place of great strategic importance for George Washington among others during the French and Indian War, the area grew into an industrial center because of the availability of coal and water power. The city turned itself around in the 1960s, 1970s, and 1980s. It cleaned itself up and became one of the most desirable places to live in the entire country.

In the 1990s, rush hour begins early. Traffic snarls as the tourist bogs down en route to the airport. The University of Pittsburgh and Carnegie Mellon University occupy a large portion of the city's territory. The University of Pittsburgh is framed by a number of excellent hospitals. Nearby residential sections feature older houses. Nowhere is a garage found—everyone parks on the street.

The streets are sometimes graced by four-wheel drives bearing the logo Emergency Physician. Young and enthusiastic emergency medicine residents are out there working with the medics in the trenches. The medics are municipal employees. People in Pittsburgh believe in EMS and do not mind paying for what is commonly thought to be an essential service. Extraordinarily sophisticated engineering concepts are applied in a readily understandable form to the problems of quality of care or quality assurance. The paramedics hold bed races in the downtown area in support of needy charities. If the past few years saw the aura of an excellent system diminished by labor shortages and salary disputes with field personnel, then more than a decade of unquestioned excellence secured for Pittsburgh an important place in American EMS history.

Two things distinguish the EMS system of Pittsburgh from many other systems. First and foremost is the extensive network of community support created through sweat, hard work, and brilliant maneuvering throughout much of the 1970s and some of the 1980s by Gerry Esposito, MPH. Esposito led the Pittsburgh system in its growth years. He forged alliances between hospitals, physicians, and industrial engineers. He built the foundation for physician training, product development, field research, and the quality assurance of active field personnel. Two of his disciples left Pittsburgh to run EMS systems in Louisville, Kentucky and Cleveland, Ohio.

The second distinguishing feature is the active involvement of physicians in supervising and/or assisting in the field delivery of emergency care. Young activist emergency care physicians dominate some of the patient care episodes in the Pittsburgh area. Intense, driven by idealism, and somehow convinced of their own infallibility, these high profile devotees of field care offer a challenge to others in the emergency care field.

The "can do" of the inhabitants of the hillocks surrounding the University of Pittsburgh is more of a trademark than the school's venerable tradition in cardiac research or medical informatics. Graduates of the Pittsburgh EMS physician training programs bring their engaging style with them to Florida and countless other places. They have also propagated the perhaps errant belief that a group of physicians could organize to give emergency medical services an added dimension in systems development or research by putting the medical doctor back in charge of organized EMS.

Pittsburgh's influence on American EMS is far greater than that city's influence in other fields. A system serving a bit more than a million people at best has positively impacted on systems serving many times that amount. EMS and EMS physicians save lives! Urban EMS is possible! But what about outside of Pittsburgh?

SEATTLE

Rain is awfully hard on people with arthritis, yet a great deal of rain can make everything appear green, lush, and beautiful. The American Northwest is dominated by major forests, mountains, sounds, and a few cities. The largest of these cities is not so much concerned with furs or lumber as with the airline industry and the very much related defense industry. Seattle is big enough to warrant several professional sports franchises. King County, Washington is also the home of one of the most noteworthy health education and paramedic franchises in American emergency care.

Cardiac Pulmonary Resuscitation training in the Seattle area is unquestionably unequalled anywhere in North America. If you were to stop two people on the street, chances are that at least one of them would be currently certified in CPR. Cardiac awareness qualifies as a major subculture in the area. It follows that Seattle is one of the most hospitable locations for cardiac-oriented EMS people to work.

This cardiac success story has some interesting wrinkles to it. The fire department, the county health department, and the University of Washington combined to forge a tradition. Preventive medicine, community health, and the notion that the general public should be the first line of defense against cardiac emergencies took root as did nowhere else. The defense line began with little children, and included a wide spectrum of citizens of all ages. Witnessed cardiac arrests had a great chance of having CPR initiated almost immediately after the patient collapsed.

Witnessed arrests were subsequently treated by paramedics who raced to the scene to intubate, to inject, or place on the tongue lifegiving drugs, and sometimes to administer an electrical current in order to "jumpstart" the patient's heart. Vasodilation or vasoconstriction might force the medics to try a number of drugs for the same call—or vary the dosage of epinephrine, depending on the apparent severity of the patient's condition. The general public living in the Seattle community worked with their high profile advanced life EMS service to wage a well thought out war on sudden cardiac death.

The results were and are spectacular. Dr. L. Bergner and Dr. M. Eisenberg, working with other physicians and non-physicians like T. Hearne, wrote a lot about what had been accomplished there. The marriage of CPR training to the general population living near the home base of the advanced life support unit came to be widely imitated elsewhere in the United States. Cardiac arrest research in New Jersey revealed the need for citizens trained in CPR to work closely in tandem with that state's hospital-directed and hospital-operated mobile intensive care units. Other states considered enlarged CPR training as the first link in wider community involvement in emergency care.

Recently, the folks in and around Seattle have been engaged in expanding the horizon of the war on sudden cardiac deaths. Intermediate EMT, a level of training normally found in the areas west and north of Illinois or the remote suburbs of New York City, has become an integral part of the caregiving scene in Seattle. EMTs are enhanced to a point where they can perform some of the procedures that paramedics have traditionally performed. This is hypothesized as being beneficial because: a) EMT-Intermediates are easier to train and maintain; and b) EMT-Intermediates are cheaper to train and less expensive to replace. Diehard advocates of the twelve-year tradition of EMT and EMT-P have been suitably miffed by Eisenberg et al.'s efforts to diversify the training levels of an urban and exurban area. EMS saves lives! And you and your neighbor should help them do it! If they ever do put defibrillators in the hands of lay people, then they will choose Seattle as the starting point.

NEW YORK

There once was a group of small islands. Civilization came, and with it came garbage. In hardly any time at all, the garbage mysteriously patched up the cracks and the watery rivulets. From this early exercise in informed sanitation, an exercise the Holland Dutch did not replicate on such a scale when dykes were employed to reclaim a large chunk of turf from the sea, arose the distinctive focal point of New York City and its surrounding suburbs—the island of Manhattan.

How does a kid from Kentucky relate to an island situated in the middle of four nearby counties? The question is compounded by the fact that Manhattan is acre after acre of buildings. And the buildings are at least ten stories tall! How can you feel more alone than when you are on a busy street at lunch hour on a work day? The hordes of eight to twelve million locals take no prisoners and very seldom offer any kind of word to strangers. It isn't personal, it is just that the scale of everything there is much too big.

Big means an abundance of everything. Consider the type of EMS system you might want to have in order to respond to 28,000 calls a week, and knowing in advance that all of them are genuinely in need of advanced or basic emergency care! The variety of patients is real, too. Poor people with track marks, hepatitis A, B, or C, and possibly menningitis are ready and waiting. Rich people with AIDS need their privacy respected as ambulances convey them to the better acute care facilities on the east side of Manahattan island.

The volume is maddening. The wide range of possibilities is stimulating for field personnel, and irritating for management personnel. Every minor mistake is blown up larger than life by the most elegant yet savage media entourage east of the Mississippi. EMS is a big fish in a huge fish bowl trying its best to get it all done.

It requires a vast number of resources to get it done. New York City has had its acute care sector serving as a backdrop for effective medicine for more than a century. New Yorkers confused many people, not the least of which were the taxation officials, through the device of maintaining the fiction that the city's Health and Hospitals Corporation was actually a fully functioning private corporation. The municipal hospital system had grown up over part of the nineteenth century and most of the twentieth century only to be hidden under a strange umbrella—an umbrella that nobody could privatize because the system gave appearance of already being private. In the period between 1964 and 1990, New York City EMS people found themselves bound up with hospitals of one type or the other. Hospitals were public or voluntary, and neither one had a whole lot of volunteers involved.

In the beginning, somewhere in a little-noted section of a sprawling city, an old and established green-pants-wearing mortuary unit mimicked the fire service as they began to fashion calls for their hearses. Not far away in lower Manhattan, Dr. W. Grace experimented with prehospital ALS. A little bit later, Dr. Boyd's gold inspired some large scale movement toward consolidating EMS resources in New York City. The green-pants-clad personnel rode ambulances and found that they were challenged by tie-wearing, white-shirt-wearing gray pants.

At the end of the seventies, the first class of paramedics was graduated in the Bronx—an area a few miles north of the towering edifices of Manhattan's Fifth Avenue or Broadway. The city's arm of emergency care rendered care for free.

EMS people could not categorize hospitals much beyond the southern end of Manhattan. They could and did devise exemplary paramedic treatment protocols. The city evolved to the point where its medical advisory committee was able to create a distinctive certification process for paramedics hoping to work in the city. The physicians on the committee could tailor the certification requirements to the real and ever-changing needs of patients in the field.

In the mid-eighties, New York City began billing for ambulance calls. The population they billed was poorer, sometimes sicker, and found it rather difficult to speak English! New York City EMS grew ever more sophisticated in order to meet the challenge. Leadership of the system passed to a former Maryland shocktrauma cutting doc by the name of Alexander Kuehl. His administration was vigorous from start to finish. Lessons learned in Nigeria, China, or North Korea found their way into the minds of captains and commanders. Soviet, British, and German physicians came together with others from this country and throughout the world to Kuehl's version of a United Nations of EMS. Sparkle, engineering, research, and adroit management didn't change the figures.

Performance figures for New York City leaped out at you from the page, the printout, or the screen. Not enough paramedics! Not enough ambulances! Incomprehensible response times! And at one point, most of the newer vehicles were not in service, while older units with 200,000 miles on them caught fire on the hottest July days that anyone could remember! The New York City EMS people were swamped.

Happily, the city's unfortunate fleet was not the only source of advanced emergency care. Years earlier, an alternative approach had been built into the advanced life support system and the basic life support system. An idea that was originally considered a mere interim measure became a fact of life during the eighties and early nineties. Private hospitals from outside the city's hospital corporation were given the responsibility for answering requests for paramedic service or 9-1-1 calls. Catholic hospitals and distinguished facilities such as Cornell Medical School's teaching affiliate, the New York Hospital, became willing and competent partners in the delivery of EMS—partners who usually, but not always, exercised the option to stay with green pants. The city periodically threatens to obliterate the partnership. After all, New York City EMS will hire enough and everything be just fine. The figures continue to leap out at you. There is a shortage of ambulances in one borough and personnel problems in a dedicated support unit. Everything will be just fine.

When the baby boomers begin to have their heart attacks, and EMS is summoned to help them, you have to wonder if they'd be better off having their attacks in Pittsburgh, Seattle, or New York. It is a fair bet that any of them might appear preferable to the idyllic burial grounds of "God's country."

CHAPTER TWELVE

───── ✳ ─────

Rural EMS—A Price You Pay for Living in God's Country?

The industrial revolution, railroads, the exodus of the well-to-do from the cities into nearby suburbs, and a large-scale industrial approach to farming known as agribusiness got out of hand between the 1870s and the 1930s. By the time the 1930s had arrived, some historians had reinterpreted the Civil War as a struggle in which the farm lost out to the city once and for all. Civilization had trumped the great outdoors in one huge cataclysmic hand.

American intellectuals had celebrated the joys of nature as early as the 1830s. A group of excessively pensive literati gathered in New England at a place known as Walden's Pond in order to reflect. A new offshoot of America's mainstream religions was born of a sermon that a man called Emerson composed there. At the height of the Vietnam War, a much different congregation gathered on a small farm in Woodstock, New York to commune with nature, each other's bodies, and, paradoxically, with recreational drugs. Smaller groupings of that type had been called "human be-ins." Hippies in the late sixties celebrated many things. Sexual fidelity, cleanliness, and acceptance of the need to grow up were not among them. Turning on, avoiding war, and the purported purity of nature were among them. But their acquiescence to pastoral settings came late, very late.

Urban and rural did engage in a heated conflagration that found expression in politics, labor relations, popular culture, and religion. In the nineteenth century, farmers moved beyond the Grange to embrace the politics of alienation found in the Populist movement. They hated banks, industrialists, and the insensivity of the federal government. As big business came to agriculture, and the federal government tinkered with whether gold or silver should warrant the validity of paper money, the farmer was squeezed into insignificance, while people like Tom Watson lost their populist manners in the racism and xenophobia of the 1890s.

A significant round in the duel between the urban and rural cultures of mainstream America took place in the 1920s. One high school science teacher lingered after finals in order to get a date with a certain graduated senior. Unfortunately, it was discovered that Mr. Scopes, a graduate of the University of Kentucky, had been teaching the godless and urban oriented doctrine of Evolutionism rather than Tennessee's preferred doctrine of Creationism. The romantic teacher was going to be put on trial. Was the world actually created in 144 hours?

America's urbane side issued a challenge. A brilliant and openly atheistic attorney came forth to defend science. Clarence Darrow had already defended two members of a religious minority in an ugly child murder case. He was now more than eager to argue that science was something clearly superior to Fundamentalism—a doctrine normally found in the nation's more countrified regions. Religions, other than the ones mired solely in human reason, were the not-so-learned adversaries of Darrow and those like him in the 1920s.

The Fundamentalists found a giant from the past to fight for the righteous and the holy against the barbarians at the gate. Former contender for the White House, William Jennings Bryan, entered the fray with God on his side. His track record was impressive. He gave a speech against the gold standard in the course of a nominating convention. Populists, farmers, and a few loyal Democrats heard him refuse to be crucified on a cross of gold and gave him the opportunity to challenge William McKinley. He ran three distinct presidential races against the Republicans and lost all of them. He wound up serving as the nation's Secretary of State under Democrat Woodrow Wilson, until his pacifist, or isolationist, feelings made him resign because he was wholly unable to endorse Wilson's drift into a purely foreign war—a war we still call World War I. The great orator was a symbol. He stood for things that rural Americans instinctively understood. He also might have stood for what used to be.

The trial was intense. Media from the more developed portions of America invaded tiny Dayton, Tennessee. In many ways, the eventual outcome was a draw. Rural literalism and urban secularism wound up in a dead heat. The teacher was convicted; however, he didn't get the gas chamber. The cultures collided. The barbarians from Chicago or New York came away with a derisive view of what seemed to be a myopic if not stupid bunch of bumpkins.

The trial confirmed some of the impudent views of well-known satirists. The spectacle convinced them that everything outside of the country's cities and suburbs was a vast and unlettered expanse of nothingness. Eastern Kentucky, the Ozarks in Arkansas, and the lands not even ten miles down the road from Memphis or Macon were without redeeming social or intellectual values.

The rural side left the proceedings pretty much believing as it had before that the damn yankee news media did not understand. Truth was at stake in their supposed "monkey trial." The foreign reporters came and saw just what they wanted and expected to see. And before the city paper final editions were cold, the rural champion died of a heart attack! Romantic accounts in the hills had him dying of a broken heart. And, to be sure, there were no CPR-trained citizens or EMTs in rural Tennessee in the 1920s! No palpable evidence of chariots landing on a junket to convey a soul lined with silver was known to have been there either.

Bryan's death marked the absolute end for rural and particularly agrarian America in the minds of many popular thinkers. It was a small matter that some of their urban counterparts were too busy guzzling bootleg gin, gambling, and cavorting in smoke-filled and dimly lit saloons. The saloons were called speakeasies and were often frequented by short-haired girls clad in outlandish make-up and short, sequined, and fringed dresses. The flapper girls danced, smoked, and boozed their way out of their "hidebound" upbringing. Like the hippies four decades later, they strove to shock, distance, and repudiate their parents.

His death paled by comparison however with the dust bowl that was created when the surface top soil of Oklahoma blew away in the 1930s. People left rural America for a supposedly better life in or very near the cities. The Okies fled to California in the 1930s. Thirty years later, numerous poor African-Americans fled Mississippi for New York, while the Scotch-Irish fled the coal mines for the perceived haven offered by Detroit. Scenic and unspoiled Vermont lost a third of its population in the sixties to outward migration.

By Lyndon Johnson's first full term in the White House, when many youth on both coasts were avidly trying to surf their boring days away, it seemed that agribusiness had won, and that farm or rural areas were destined to be underpopulated. During the Vietnam War, it became clear that the issue wasn't quite settled after all. People in Washington and Oregon were getting most unwelcome permanent exiles from California. They were not the rural poor in search of a new life; they were people in search of serenity and the good life as it was found in the country. The principle attraction was that rural just wasn't urban. People started commuting two hours or more down the interstates from Easton, Pennsylvania or Sparta, New Jersey to Metropolitan New York. It was worth it to raise kids beside the Delaware River or in midst of miniature corn, cherrystone tomatoes, and dairy cattle.

Of course, nothing was permanent. Noise, pollution, and drug dealers all came to play havoc with the middle class parent's escapist fantasies. Still, everything was a matter of degree. It would take a while for a city to catch up to them. It would take longer for the motor vehicle accident statistics on the affected interstates to reflect unexpected growth by an upward bulge.

The cities did not stop growing. The inner core began to suffer here and there from traces of decay—a decay that when left unattended would eventuate in outright rot or what later became the bombed-out section of New York City known as the South Bronx. People left the city to live in the suburbs. Some of them in turn moved more than seventy miles from their place of work to escape suddenly blighted suburban societies. People ran away from other people only to encounter other people. It was a one way revolving door. Some rural Americans took root in the city. Many urban Americans chose to live and, if possible, work in the suburbs or the wondrously restful country.

The shock was less acute in Nevada or Arizona than it was in Manchester, New Hampshire or Washington Township, New Jersey. You couldn't run away! Paul Revere and the Raiders even had a popular song that proclaimed that sentiment as it applied to drugs as an escape. You had to get a kick somehow! The air was clean, and for a decade or so the water was too! Not to worry if there were few public health or public safety resources. Old folks lived longer in the clean air. People attended houses of worship regularly. Country musicians intoned several anthems to the joys of rustic purity. Some of them were originally fifties rock singers or folk artists in Greenwich Village, Manhattan, or New York City.

If someone: a) bled out without ever seeing an ambulance; or b) got the ambulance but didn't have a Mt. Vernon style rural trauma center to go to; and c) wound up stabilized in the sticks well enough to permit transfer to a more specialized faraway center; only to d) wind up as the source of a few donated organs; well then, that is the price you had to pay for living in god's country.

Rural EMS finally added up to a situation where there were too few resources dedicated to comparatively rare, but sometimes god awful serious, accidental injuries. There were even a few recalcitrants who remained in the sticks after qualifying for Social Security, or folks in their forties who persisted in vacationing there. Both types had heart attacks on occasion. If the demand for EMS increased even slightly, rural EMS found it difficult to meet the need for added resources.

If the crew does not sleep in at a fixed point, or roll by at an established time on an extended fly car route, then the time between the receipt of the call and the actual dispatching of an EMS unit of some kind is horribly long. If the dispatched unit takes at least eleven minutes to arrive on the scene, then numerous algorithms about "do no harm" to viable patients go by the boards. If time on scene and transport time to the hospital consume even more time, then what is the use of a golden hour (the sixty to seventy minutes in which shock in trauma patients may be reversed) let alone a defibrillator? The odds in god's country seem to warrant a protocol for divine intervention.

The number of personnel volunteering for rural EMS in the 1990s is not sufficient to get around the need for such a protocol. Rural EMS services in the forests of Northern New York do not have enough paramedics, intermediate-EMTs, EMTs, or first responders. Classes are hard to find, and they require long drives to attend. The weather can seriously hinder a forty-mile trip to school on an unlit

two-lane blown-over state road. Despite the hardships involved, Pennsylvania and New York, among other places, have come up with
rural emergency training schemata. The farm medics come to know
things that grizzled and stonefaced veterans of Harlem or the battlefields near UCLA and USC haven't the slightest hope of knowing
without experiencing them first-hand. A barbed wire laceration
exposes a farmer over the age of fifty to both organic and synthetic
fertilizers. Medics from Idaho and New York could trade jobs for a
week in order to have the basis for an honest understanding of one
another's stations in life. The stations are not the same.

The constant din of highly intense calls is decidedly unequal to
the sporadic but potentially complicated gnawing at your heels
found in the American outback. Some believe the rural regions left
in the country could be more uniformly covered by a thin ocean of
forty-hour prepared first responders. A large fraction of these responders will be still further prepared by a short course in the use of
the not quite smart defibrillators. Still others believe that the requirements for volunteer rescue personnel everywhere must be
lessoned. A minority in Montana and Virginia have tried to
modularize training for skills such as those contained in PHTLS or
BTLS via the use of videotapes throughout a region and the sched-
uling of practical exams on a regular basis in central locations.

It may be in fact that EMS folks can overcome at least some of
the very real obstacles posed by living and providing EMS in god's
country. Reason, logic, and a touch of science may go a long way
toward lowering the enormously high price associated with delivering and receiving emergency medical care in rural America. The
1980s have seen the logistical problems worsen and a few clever
solutions received only tentatively by the EMS industry as a whole.

Rural EMS systems are less likely to be tax supported than
almost any other kind. Elite professional services or slavishly dedicated volunteers have to fill the bill. Some more learned appraisals
of staffing, dispatch, and ambulance placement difficulties may be
developed in the 1990s. The Darrows of this decade are sure of it.
Maybe the present-day Bryans would allow as how learned appraisals
can be useful at times—if only as an alternative mode of thought.
Most Americans still put their trust in science. EMS personnel are
very prominent among them. Science can be useful. It can also be
downright disappointing (Mr. Scopes never did get to date the girl).

CHAPTER THIRTEEN

―――――― ✳ ――――――

Technology—EMS and Science

At the close of the eighteenth century, many serious and influential minds in Western Europe chose to abandon Catholicism or Protestantism, together with all the warfare each had caused, in favor of reason. Emotional impulses and unstructured creative moments were suspect. One or two eccentrics found that they were incarcerated in mental institutions. In the elite circles, finite mathematicians given to neologisms became dominant, as informed minds wondered out loud how it was they knew what they knew. Monads, categorical imperatives, and a fervent belief that almost anything could be arrived at through an enlightened, purely reasoned out logical process. Humans were capable of discovering an objective truth nearly as powerful as the one theologians had been using to foment bloody wars for many years. The period is usually commended by historians as a time of enlightenment.

It is a watershed in western culture. In the following century, reason took a beating in light of a number of mostly secular yet democratic rebellions against ruling European monarchs in Europe and Central and South America. The best of all possible truths ended up in bloodshed just like the holy terrors it had done. The application of pure reason to political life had begun to come apart at the seams.

Later in the nineteenth century, radical thinkers drew on the secularized cult the sum and substance of ostensibly social theories of the human race's place in the universe. Some went so far as to reject traditional societal structures entirely. Karl Marx, Georges Sorel, and the makers of modern Belgium all aspired to plan a new universe—a universe that came to pass in England, Sweden, and to a lesser extent, the Soviet Union. In the twentieth century, people like the British author and philospher George Orwell embraced this radical anarcho-syndicalist perspective on the battlefields of Spain in the 1930s. He came to revile the lack of any kind of structure as something evil. Politics and social theories were not the best arenas in which to showcase the merits of reason as the natural religion.

The nineteenth and twentieth centuries did experience the rise of a much less disturbing offshoot of the rationalist faith. In the laboratory, or the hills of Kentucky where a method for refining steel was perfected, everywhere was found a host of enthusiasts for the cult of progress. The human race could apply reason to the problems of this world and daily life and then go on to solve them. Look what Pasteur did for milk processing! Look what mass production did in the area of logistics (shoes, pants, etc.) for the beleagured soldiers on the northern side of the Civil War! Look what the managerial nuances required for that task did to the earliest proto-types for 1990's MBA executives! But also look at what rapid-fire weapons did for the Prussians a few years later against the French!

The cure and prevention of disease had to follow. Technology and the application of reason in pursuit of truth would conquer diptheria just as surely as it had brought about steel production, steam-driven naval vessels and ocean liners, and all the things you could dream of in a modern progressive society. Reason might even prove that a small circle of British white males, living nervously at the turn of the nineteenth century, were inherently superior to most other humans—and the proof itself would come, if at all, by means of a newly minted discipline known as statistics. This new discipline could rectify or justify the then popular notion that there was indeed a white man's burden.

Objective truth was and is something best left in the eyes of its beholder. But by 1920, you might wind up ninety-five percent or ninety-nine percent sure that what you saw was not a mere fluke, accident, or chance event! And progress was almost around the corner? Some people were so sure of it that they got political about it and soon called the breakaway splintered beliefs by the name of positivism.

In the early part of the twentieth century, learning and research did in fact advance immunology and public health light years ahead of where each had been up to that time. People genuinely came to believe that all good things came to those who researched carefully and experimented scientifically. One by one diseases that had been the scourge of the young were eliminated as meaningful threats. The battle was and is ongoing. Polio was all but eradicated shortly before John F. Kennedy came to office. Smallpox ceased to be a problem a little more than a decade later. Some EMS people cherish the gut-level conviction that trauma is a disease as well. It follows for them that the functional equivalent of immunization or a flat-out cure will be found for it. Scientists control disease, or so they'll tell you. Science saves lives—sometimes.

Science was not a widespread obsession until the cold warriors lost their composure and became panic-stricken because the godless Communists were as of 1957 much more rational, positivist, or what have you than the Americans had thus far managed to be. The red menace had a satellite in orbit around the earth. The scientific community was instantly rediscovered, reborn, and enlarged. Massive funding came to the rescue. America had to catch up and did so in short order. Setting as a goal the placement of American astronauts on the moon in just a decade was the height of ambition. The goal was realized dramatically.

Science grant monies were available to universities as never before. Research into defense-related fields became commonplace from the sixties right on through to the 1990s. EMS flourished during a portion of that same period. The scientific climate of opinion, coupled with the popular article of faith that science was an American redoubt against both Communist and clinical threats, served the first EMTs and paramedics well. A residue of "can do" combined with an earnest certitude that the scientific method was the only recourse made for elaborate, ambitious, prolix, unreadable, and downright arcane scientific literature about the whys and wherefores of a young field.

NHTSA 403 monies and Dr. Boyd's cache of 1205 dollars fueled much in the way of legitimate research. The dollars also fueled speculative nonsense that deigned to establish how many EMS residents could dance on the head of a pin in contrast to the same equation when applied to urban paramedics or EMT-Ds in the rural midwest. Critics of Dr. Boyd's flamboyant regime seized on what appeared to be a learned version of the pork barrel fiasco. The NHTSA 403 projects were generally compromises with state-level interested parties or awards to irrefutable scholars in Pittsburgh, Maine, or Wisconsin. The popular misconception that this somehow conveyed a greater legitimacy on NHTSA's overall approach to everything was and is a matter for one's own individual interpretation. In general, it has to be said there is no preponderance of scientific evidence that favors the research that Leo Schwartz and DOT's Paul Levy sanctioned over the work blessed by Dr. Boyd and Dr. Larry Rose of the National Center for Health Services Research.

Technocratic innovation and an engineering slant at times produced research that proved that EMS in and of itself had little or no impact on the problems it addressed. The public health and DEMS sides of the hall had engendered analyses that harked back to the eighteenth century "how do I know what I know" school of thought. Basic life support bordering on "scoop and run" (immediately loading a patient into the ambulance and providing very little care en route to the hospital) saved as many or more patients than paramedics could in the late seventies.

How do you prove that a system works before it is finished? How can you get a large number of people to pay cash up front for a system that was largely unproven except for a few demonstration projects and Dr. Boyd's experiment in and around Mt. Vernon, Illinois? Do you demonstrate that the structure of a system was at least in place? Do you then go on to suggest that a systematic process was functioning in a fairly predictable manner? Given both of those assumptions, could you demonstrate conclusively that EMS made a tangible difference, had an impact, or saved lives?

From 1964 through the 1990s, American EMS people took a shot at evaluating the effectiveness of emergency care delivery systems. EMS evaluation research perennially chased after the health care delivery equivalent of the Holy Grail. Hundreds of evaluation specialists raced to discover the answer. Zeal in some quarters and stoical reserve in other quarters led directly to huge printouts, complex computers, dubious or imperfectly collected data, trenchant resistance from affected parochial interests, and troubles on the inside. EMS evaluation people were resented if not outwardly despised by EMS field people. One group did the work! The other smaller group invalidated it or at least failed to keep an implied promise to validate some of it. Despite Herculean efforts, and not a few isolated successes (especially in Illinois, Iowa, and the Oakland area of California), the case for an economic and clinically imposing advanced life support system remains unmade in the 1990s.

The case for a much less expensive and clearly less glamorous basic life support system was made by Dr. Boyd's regions and a few of the NHTSA-inspired researchers. At present, EMS planners and system builders are still trying to ascertain how much is enough. Their unwritten supposition is that ALS is cost prohibitive. Some go so far as to discount ALS as clinical overkill. On the other hand, BLS is affordable yet a bit too unskilled. Analysts contemplate studying various innovative methods to fill in the middle ground or gray area. Will EMTs with defibrillators make up some of the gap? Should more intermediate level EMTs be allowed to intubate or give intravenous fluids? Careful analysis *might* yield answers to these questions.

It is likely that the questions will be posed in the context of quality assurance or quality improvement—both elements of managerial sciences imported from the computer and fire service industries. These organizational focuses are predicated upon risk management considerations. Reducing the negative exposures that could end up in litigation is something EMS people consider highly important. Reducing cost through greater efficiency is the ultimate survivalist ethic for a health care delivery organization, while the system itself is the outcome of the health delivery experiment.

During the last 110 years, there have been a few retired positivists who have dared to step away from a natural or overly rational view of learning. They generally offer the most fundamental of criticisms: any discipline that has become caught up in its own internal debates over what methods to use in conducting a study has ceased making an active contribution to anyone or anything in the real world. While this particular bromide was intended as a sort of backhanded edification for American sociologists, historians, and psychologists suffering from the conviction that they were linear descendants of Herbert Spencer, William Graham Sumner,

Auguste Comte, and Max Weber, it has a bearing on EMS as a learned discipline as well. You cannot go on endlessly promising answers, while continually haggling over questions if you are to have any hope of a greater audience or wider support.

EMS folks have learned to do more focused research since the advent of the 1970s. Studies in EMS emulate the scientific methods that a chemist or smart bomb developer might use. Procedures and drugs are evaluated over time—time that usually consists of clinical trials conducted over three to five years. Some of the cardiac kids among EMS researchers have wound up believing that certain levels of cardiac life support require long term longitudinal analysis to determine their effectiveness. Some of the trauma researchers now feel that traumatic injuries susceptible of impact by organized EMS systems must be studied with reference to similar injuries in the overall (a.k.a. parent) population. How many people are likely to suffer a fractured hip among those over the age of sixty-five? How many actually did suffer such injuries among those treated by EMS in the field? How many were seen by EMS in the emergency room of the Trauma Intensive Care Unit only? (Did the system make an impact on crude mortality and morbidity profiles for the area that it served?)

It is not a matter of EMS digging into minutiae. It is a matter of EMS breaking out in several directions, away from strictly critical care research. The disease process, the population it affects, and the measures EMS people use to deal with both of these factors are the key elements of learned science as it applies to EMS. It is a science destined to grow in the public health, public safety, cardiac, and trauma directions after a long internship under the veneer of more established bodies of knowledge (e.g., nursing research, program evaluation research, and business oriented qualitative analysis).

The cost benefit associated with various levels of care and training has been established. The probable contraindications for the use of MAST garments or certain drugs (e.g., manitol) are considered as documented truths. Detailed investigation examines what will work and what will not work. In the process of doing so, EMS researchers establish a floating decimal estimate of how much is enough.

Telecommunications is another area in which science has made a tremendous impact on EMS from 1964 through the 1990s. EMS people have gone from buried phone lines dedicated for their use at a minimum of five dollars per foot in the 1970s, to using cellular phones to avoid all but the most imperative radio communications. Computers that fill a building and cost well over half a million dollars have been combined with small portable laptops carried by ambulance crews, or small computers built into the ambulances, to give EMS people a brand new world.

Under ideal circumstances, medical direction and dispatch information are merely points on the same end of a two-way street. The crews and the rig they call home show up on the grids of electronic maps. A precise location for each unit flashes on and off. The signal from the flashing light changes once a crew has taken more than six to ten minutes on scene. This is especially true of an advanced life support call.

Vehicle locating and resource coordination has been raised to the level of an art form in Atlanta and part of Virginia as of 1990. It gives EMS much more flexibility in dealing with major accidents and other mass casualty situations. EMS folks have a sense of being in control. A fleet of units can be utilized at its optimal level of functioning. It is expensive. Many times, it requires pooling dollars with public safety providers beset by similar communications problems. Sometimes, as the daily EMS drama plays itself out in the large-scale world of urban and exurban EMS, science does make a huge difference, such as every time a crew person uses a phone or a microphone.

There are other scales. Some EMS personnel are not completely sold on the virtues of either technocracy or scientific research as a major part of the answers to their very particular needs. They subscribe to a faith that is largely devoid of reason. It has long been their hope that they might yet purify impersonal EMS bureaucracies by example.

CHAPTER FOURTEEN

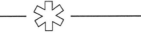

The Vollies

In the early seventies, the popular rock group, Jefferson Airplane, used the image of volunteers scurrying to save a fallen America as the motif for what became a best-selling album called *Volunteers for America*. While Dr. Boyd and the wide array of elements that grew evermore vocal in frank opposition to him contended for a stranglehold on EMS truth, rockers who worked within a millieu that featured tripping out on alcohol, drugs, very recreational if much too impersonal sex, and a frank fascination with the power that made them modern-day prophets, used the image of the volunteer to sell records and to instill the need for a national revolution in many a youthful heart. Volunteering is an unusual thing for people to do. Being a vollie entails belonging to a subculture and acting like a radical.

In the nineteenth century, a small and highly motivated portion of the population abandoned unsafe mills and harsh labor conditions to form colonies in Indiana, Kentucky, New York, and New Hampshire. This escape from the evils of a mercenary and polluted world had its secular and religious counterparts in the 1960s and the early 1970s. The average American living in the 1840s rejected the idea of building your own world to replace the one that bothers you so much and so often with its imperfections. The "can do" Americans were not inclined to take up residence in the Haight-Ashbury section of San Francisco or the East Village area of Lower

Manhattan on the opposite coast. The nineteenth century malcontents could vent their considerable frustrations by means of racist or nativist organizations, fraternal organizations that often doubled as exclusivist organizations, the workingperson's unions, or their rural equivalent—the Grange. The twentieth century malcontents living in "can do" America had a much broader range of outlets available to them.

Between 1964 and 1974, many distinguished and salaried people decided to destroy the "bombs before breakfast" or "whatever is best for business" value system of America. They failed. They did offer an escapist fantasy that surpassed anything the local acid and speed dealer had to sell you. The allure came from the notion that you could out-and-out reject almost everything and start from scratch. There is a fine line between innovation and psychosis. Dropping out meant, and still means in the 1990s, that you are willing to walk along that line as though it were some sort of mystical tightrope. Obliterating American culture was only one avenue of the many beckoning in "can do" America.

There were the usual amount of lodge organizations, veterans organizations, volunteer fire departments that were part public safety and part social group, political organizations like the Young Americans for Freedom or the Students for a Democratic Society, older political organizations like the Americans for Democratic Action and its often incognito opponent, the Silent Majority, and there were a comparative handful of folks who got into EMS on a volunteer basis. Maybe most of the Americans living in the sixties and early seventies felt that the organization of industry and labor solely to make a buck was somehow ignoble. If a service is truly an essential one, then it follows that someone who performs it should be either altruistic and independently wealthy or salaried at a level appropriate enough to keep valuable personnel for ten to twenty years. Police departments and major fire departments may be operated as though each were part of a private concern, but it is rare indeed that you find a volunteer officer or a major urban fire station operated on a strictly volunteer basis.

Emergency medical services do not enjoy universal acceptance as one of the essential elements in American life. Forty years ago, haphazard arrangements were the rule instead of the exception. No arrangements of any kind at all might prevail in the more rural areas. Providing an unaccepted yet deadly serious service to the community required a unique group of individuals.

This group might have sprung up from concerns issuing forth among volunteer firefighters. The local American Legion or the local Veterans of Foreign Wars Post might have elected to evince their civic-mindedness by putting it on the line. People with time on their hands away from their real jobs could have pooled their efforts and combined to form an organization. Doing so ordinarily meant that they gave ten to twenty hours over and above the forty hours they customarily gave to the work week. The added hours could total much more than twenty if they weren't careful.

The time was given willingly, as if it were being given by radical or revolutionary visionaries pursuing a vision that almost no one else understood. Winning other people over to these noble visions added an extra dimension to their lives. Nobody should doubt that the visionaries were pretty darn sacred—even if they did say so themselves. They observed so much more intensely than many others. Their obligation to render high quality prehospital emergency care was posited as a moral absolute. Their compliance with such an absolute was to be taken as an article of faith. Measuring compliance with field algorithms vital to such a faith was of course their own prerogative.

The radicals of this world often find themselves driven out of the mainstream of a given society. They are made to go it alone—as alone as the Pilgrims were when they landed on Plymouth Rock. They conquer virgin turf as the Mormons did under tremendous duress in nineteenth century Utah. They fill gaps that nobody else would or could fill. The experience bonds them together and so they form a large family. After several years of securing deliverance in a much vaunted promised land, the family develops some inherent discord—young and new versus old and seasoned. As New Light Protestants in Kentucky and Tennessee do when a dispute arises, or as a professional sports franchise is likely to do if a strong lead on a better location comes to light, the discordant visionaries split away from old loyalties and go their separate ways.

Have you ever seen a town with a population of 2,000 and a transient population of maybe 20,000 more on the weekends being served by three distinct volunteer rescue units? The people with a house in the country are undoubtedly very much impressed and the locals somewhat bemused. Maybe the heroic visions of yesteryear have misfired? The volunteer ethic has mutated in the far reaches of a lake country situated less than two hours from a major city!

In the narrow valleys of Kentucky, groups drop out of certain factions of the New Light church in order to form the second, third, and fourth factions of the New Light church—and the congregations follow in rapid succession, taking from ten to thirty years to make a full cycle. Some of the smaller dropout newer light religionist groups are forced to close. There is a dearth of properly motivated people willing to give freely of their hearts and their time. It may just be that some factions will merge with break-offs of other factions in order to go their own way. Under such circumstances, the old ones will endeavor to grit their teeth and joyfully receive all those prodigal sons and daughters. College fraternities and sororities often experience one-way shakeouts in which juniors and seniors attached to the wrong clique depledge and disassociate themselves from the winning clique after an election of officers. The religious and social organizations in contemporary America are prone to a certain amount of internal cell division.

Volunteer emergency medical service organizations are most definitely social in character. In parts of Pennsylvania, during the 1980s, new EMTs and paramedics were initiated into the fight against unnecessary death through the expedient of hazing—a ritual lasting for as long as two years. In other parts of the Northeast, again during the liberated 1980s, blatant sexism was manifest. Women did not have to trail the men by ten paces. They did have to forego using practical skills and clinical background knowledge in deference to older or at least gruffer men. Both the skills and the knowledge had been acquired in classes taken together with male EMT or paramedic students. Typical of the irrational extreme of such bantering was the forced analogy between the Women's Army Corps members of the 1940s and the streetsmart ladies working in EMS. The idea was that streetwise women were possibly prone to an alternative sexual orientation. It was as if stereotypes would serve to hold the line against the sexual integration of the older congregations of the volunteer EMS faith.

As time wore on, and the economy wound down, the vollies sometimes lost out for the following reasons:

a) people had to take two jobs to pay their bills;

b) baby boom parents had a number of commitments associated with their children who played sports or appeared in plays during junior high and high school;

c) the vollies themselves decided they liked EMS well enough to become volunteer paramedics for a scheduled service;

d) the once dedicated vollies decided to become paid EMS professionals on a full time basis and were prohibited from doing that and serving on a volunteer squad in the same town while off duty;

and, most onerously,

e) the vollies worried openly that they did not have the time to maintain either EMT or paramedic skills.

Volunteer EMS in the 1990s is much different from the type of volunteer emergency care available in 1974 or 1984. Even in suburban areas, where daytime medics in the big city double as vollie crew chiefs in their home areas at night, the numbers aren't there. Proud and well-established volunteer organizations are staffed by paid municipal and public-safety inspired EMTs or medics during the daylight hours. A fanatical commitment to more and better training isn't there either. Many who felt a sense of responsibility toward the individual patient have aged a bit since 1964 and the early training experiments some seven to nine years later. The old religionists are ready to become patients themselves in a few years.

Young blood has mixed with some older blood to form volunteer EMS organizations that bear little resemblance to the storied past. If some are poorly trained or not recently certified, then they grow up to be individuals with a certain haughtiness—a haughtiness that is most evident when they are busily swearing on some holy honor that they just didn't have time. Computerized tutorials and videotapes are used in the Big Sky Country and in Virginia to mitigate time management problems posed by volunteers in contemporary society. This serves to keep well-intentioned EMS folks from falling into this "pity me" trap. But what can be done about the notion that caring for someone is in reality doing them a favor?

If EMS is in some ways a religion, and it might be better if it were not, then vollie EMS can be one of the most purified sects ever to try bringing new light to emergency care. The vollie has filled the care gap because no one else could or would. The vollie gives a labor of love to save other human beings. Mistakes were and still are forgiven because the deceased or maimed patient's family takes into account the selfless spirit of the volunteer caregivers involved. Something was better than nothing, and something tends to be a moot point.

The late eighties have seen the enthusiastic adoption of these principles on the part of several state-level EMS offices. The inability of volunteer organizations to retain full compliments of active members has contributed to the development of a large number of surrogates. The basic level of care in the Northeast may soon be the forty-hour first responder with or without the defibrillator. In the Northwest, the Intermediate EMT may yet prove to be a low cost susbstitute for the paramedic. EMTs may have to grow accustomed to refreshing their training by challenging modules of the practical and written exams that usually came only after a twenty-eight-hour refresher course. Magazines and trade newspapers might even succeed in generating interest in relevant Continuing Education Units given by extension—an extension that less than twenty percent of the states approved of in 1990. How much time does it take to reflect a bit and then fill out a stimulating short exam in the magazine or the paper?

Less is more. One state went so far as to conclude that volunteers needed to know appreciably less skills than the professional EMTs do, and so they should learn less. The DOT-NHTSA people are trying to strike a responsive chord among basic life support caregivers by overhauling training standards to reflect what EMTs actually do in the field. The grants are out. By the early to mid '90s, EMTs will benefit from a more reality-based corpus of knowledge.

Clearly, governments at all levels have grown pretty zealous about preserving the volunteer tradition. It's a small wonder too, since professional emergency care personnel availing themselves of non-abbreviated and labor-intensive programs for Basic, Intermediate, and Advanced Life Support are *de facto* cost prohibitive in the small cities, small suburbs, and rural areas. Are vollies and fly cars the best anyone can hope for during the next decade?

A large number of incentives have been put together in order to entice the ever diminishing number of vollies to stay on the job. Jackets, mugs, tax shelters, and a license to practice EMS at some sort of level all come with the 1990s franchise for your local Plymouth Rock. The idea that you are accountable to those on that rock with you and to them alone works for some people better than others. Volunteers can maintain professional standards of care, but they don't have to do it.

The vollies have been an essential component of American EMS since 1964. While public health and public safety were turfing it out, and categorical medicine vacillated between the cardiac kids and the knife and gun clubs, the first to fifteenth new light true EMS congregations plugged the many gaps formed as a direct result of discord, indecisiveness, and the failure of the more established groups to detail the mission of EMS in concrete terms. American EMS would have been virtually invisible without these radicals. Whether they will continue to play a major or leading role in the future is open to question. The question harks back to management concerns, economic considerations, and the marginal possibility that EMS will somehow achieve a working consensus about what it is all about and what it ought to be doing.

CHAPTER FIFTEEN

Renaissance?

Many of the children born during the baby boom period have gone to work in EMS. The fortysomethings get misty-eyed when they recall Dr. Boyd's magnificent effort to set the world of acute care medicine on its ear. A national crusade changed their lives and inspired them to remain in EMS despite far more lucrative job offers from hospitals or nursing homes. The ignominious collapse of the Title 12 Program found them defiantly refusing to accept the fact that a systematic approach to the organization of emergency care delivery systems was, as of 1982, pretty much a lost cause.

EMS is not unique in this respect. A number of successful programs such as the neighborhood health centers or the earliest forms of health maintenance organizations bit the dust between 1964 and the early eighties. Health care in the popular mind became synonymous with waste—waste that meant too many needless hysterectomies or extensive study yielding too few results with regard to cancers. If Americans felt impotent in the face of the fall of Saigon or the parading of hostages in Teheran, and if they felt all the more like the citizens of a banana republic as foreign car manufacturers overthrew the once proud carmaker titans of Detroit, then they found the federal government to be a viable scapegoat with which to expiate these failures and other sins.

Johnson gave us Medicare. Nixon did many things, both good and bad, but with respect to health care it can be said that he perpetuated most of the "big government is good government" liberal mythology that had its origins in the first hundred days of Franklin Roosevelt's presidency in the 1930s. Gerald Ford began to chip away at that mythology. Jimmy Carter's fiscal conservatism gutted it. It was left to Ronald Reagan to apply the *coup de grace* by shifting the overall federal emphasis away from social programs in the general direction of long-neglected defense programs such as weapons development.

Under Reagan, many federal functions were farmed out to the states. Other functions fed off of unprecedented interest in, and participation from, private industry. Accordingly, EMS standards were supposed to evolve from a group process comprised of EMS industry providers and consumers. Many of these interested parties faced real economic perils if the wrong standards were approved and came to have the impact of a law.

EMS has gone through the past quarter of a century riding a seesaw. By 1990, EMS had a most interesting relationship with the federal government. DEMS and NHTSA had both nurtured EMS in their own separate ways. Which side had won? It seems that EMS must be a social program because of its direct linkage to Medicare and Medicaid in both the hospital and prehospital phases of care. EMS can also double as a defense program because of the backup role that trauma centers and burn programs play during wartime. Unfortunately, EMS is not a burning national priority in 1990. The cardiac kids go without twelve leads or beta blockers. Little research is done on the best way to reach and treat conditions that comprise more than forty percent of the advanced life support patient mix in most major systems.

The trauma junkies do better in the area of research dollars. They benefit from a prehospital focus on injury control (a.k.a. prevention). Some of this is covertly led by the scant DOT federal advocates that remain in Washington, DC. Appropriate reimbursement for multi-trauma cases is much less well-supported at the federal level. Paying for the care of patients who haven't yet lived long enough to reach their sixties has been shunted gracefully to the individual states. How many sixty-five-year-old crack dealers packing nine millimeter weapons have you run into lately? Who has the money to cover the costs run up by the younger members of the Knife and Gun Club? It would take a mere three hundred complicated trauma cases to exhaust the monies being considered in the Senate for the purposes of inspiring a trauma-EMS system on a nationwide basis beginning in 1991. (See below.)

It would seem then that events have fallen into place about the way Nixon thought they should when he vetoed the first version of an EMS Systems Act back in 1973. Was Moynihan mistaken? EMS is a state and local problem. If your state's share of the one thousand points of light glow brighter, well then you are relatively well-off. If the residue from the DEMS days is spent, and little interest in EMS persists apart from the attendance of state functionaries at little-noted meetings, then big trouble may yet come your way. After 1982, the national government abdicated all formal EMS systems development responsibilities.

In nearly sixty percent of the states, this retreat translated into no trauma centers and little prospect of any such expensive centers. The federal and state government revenue schemes so popular during Lyndon Baines Johnson's day and age were no longer a factor for EMS folks in 1990. A trauma bill was passed in 1990. It avoided President Bush's veto. The bill might result in a passing through of a small amount of monies—monies particularly slated for states with next to nothing in the way of trauma-EMS systems. There has been a great deal of reluctance to compel these delinquent states to build trauma centers lest they lose federal highway construction dollars. President Bush offered the promise of a carrot and not even the hint of a stick as 1990 drew to a close.

In the fall of that year, physicians who were trained in wars located in Los Angeles, Washington, DC, and New Orleans, among other places, were sent to Saudi Arabia to help out with penetrating traumas—traumas more prevalent in our urban combats than in what used to be West Germany or what still is South Korea. Hospitals were alerted stateside. Professional and volunteer EMS providers were issued call notices for their patient transport responsibilities. The grizzled veterans on the verge of burnout and the ever-zealous vollies stood ready to ferry wounded military personnel from drop-off points to the hospitals comprising the nation's acute care sector.

Yellow ribbons signified cautious steps toward a "can do" approach to war, acute care, traumatology, and the idea of America itself. The fear of failure ebbed a bit as the throngs of peace pickets never really appeared. A morose fixation on a long black wall began to diminish as well. POW-MIA flags in front of countless municipal buildings blended into a background of yellow bows. American flags were everywhere. For the first time since 1968, flag-waving patriotism was not viewed as jingo, ultrarightist, or species of rank foolishness worthy only of the uneducated.

The orgy of introspection that began thirteen years earlier was ending. Maybe America's wounded pride would heal. Private industry could be a partner with the government in something other than the manufacture of the most excellent high technology weapons. Privitization of emergency medical service systems in the states of Washington and Florida carried within it the hope that EMS could be all-encompassing and efficient at one and the same time. And above all, myopic or parochial perspectives would vanish in the face of some larger, yet to be defined American identity. Idle albeit constructive speculation will not bring back Dr. Boyd's national EMS office. It cannot revitalize Dr. Boyd's low-key yet highly effective rivals at DOT either.

EMS can impact on medical emergencies. EMS folks scramble to meet the needs of cardiac patients who are urgently in need of critical care medicine. Trauma cases may yet have whole systems built around them—just like in Illinois eighteen years ago. But they may only be trauma systems—systems that leave little room for planning to meet the needs of other patients!

Can America foster a rebirth of the spirit that gave rise to a lively, almost surging EMS revolution in the years prior to 1982? Is the EMS field in imminent danger of being unified? Have the four threads of public health, public safety, cardiac, and trauma been woven together to form a much stronger thread suitable for use on the toughest of jobs?

Any new efforts to revolutionize acute or prehospital care would run smack into the inherent contradictions that paralyze and often polarize emergency care. Everybody may stand a chance of needing EMS. Nobody can precisely define EMS. EMS people do know the elation that comes from a definite save. Reaching out into an apparent void and bringing a person back from nothingness rivals the birth of your own child as a natural high. EMS people deliver other people from death or the lasting effects of an injury. EMS people are delivered from an otherwise meaningless existence by doing their lifesaving bit. EMS people have tremendously meaningful work.

Since 1964, EMS people have failed to communicate the peculiar rapture that comes with what the street medics and the EMTs call the "jazz." EMS comes with its own mind-expanding mushrooms—and only those who are laying on hands can hope to partake of their hidden mysteries. This makes EMS people quite special. It also renders it incomprehensible to mild-mannered and unassuming people in the buttondown reality of mainstream America.

Part of the failure to communicate stems from a different set of experiences that weren't shared and the divergent mindsets this lack of sharing produces. Another part of the EMS identity problem comes from the images the various tribes have of one another. EMS is confused. EMS is hard to identify. How would anyone of consequence go about supporting it?

Hospital, fire department, high performance system, municipal, and/or vollie agencies employ medics, EMT-Intermediates, and plain old EMTs to deliver lifesaving emergency care to traumas, cardiacs, and everyone else (e.g., medical emergencies, especially respiratories) in order to maintain the public health in the interests of public safety. Subscription anyone? The public health authorities incompletely regulate the reimbursement given to the agencies involved in both the hospital and the prehospital phases of emergency care. Public safety officials in DC are increasingly less involved with EMS on a direct basis despite the fact that most EMS providers train under standards mandated in their respective states under the auspices of the time-honored Department of Transportation. Who's in charge? What is it all about? Could you hope to give a straight answer to a five-year-old? A fifteen-year-old? A fifty-year-old?

Until straight and direct answers can be found for the myriad riddles that blur the "who does what for whom" of organized emergency care, and until EMS people can focus on what is usable and what was awfully stupid about their own not-so-distant past, an EMS systems renaissance is a childish fantasy at best. A decade ago, you could sit rival agency heads together at a dinner table, and after hours of searching, you would find just one thing they could agree upon without reservation. Nobody on the public health side would dispute the public safety side's contention that ambulances should be easy to identify anywhere you might go in the United States. They were partially white. An Aesculapian Star was centered on the side. The rigs would stand out in a traffic jam, especially in the daytime, because they were trimmed in a shade called Omaha Orange. The nineties may be a period in which EMS people learn to paint patient care needs with one color and have the rest of the American population genuinely appreciate why. Trim paint on the nation's fleet of ambulances in Jimmy Carter's day is a heck of a strange monument to EMS harmony since 1964. A newer monument might express just as much universality without losing the concept of an enlarged focus. The four threads might be blended into something bigger and better to the point where they are no longer distinguishable from other factors within the political economy of health care in the United States. And then, as is true now: sometimes you win one, other times you lose one, but you get up and dress for them all, and still the beat goes on.

Index